THOSE WERE THE DAYS

THOSE WERE THE DAYS

Seán Power

editor

GILL & MACMILLAN

Gill & Macmillan Ltd
Goldenbridge
Dublin 8
with associated companies throughout the world
© Introduction and Selection Seán Power 1995
0 7171 2384 7

Design and print origination by
O'K Graphic Design, Dublin
Printed by
ColourBooks Ltd, Dublin

A catalogue record is available for this book from the
British Library.

1   3   5   4   2

This book is dedicated to
Ciarain Malone

CONTENTS

INTRODUCTION

In early 1992 I called to the Children's Cancer Hospital in Crumlin. I had gone to talk with Dr Fin Breatnach, Consultant Paediatric Oncologist, and when our meeting finished, he introduced me to his sick little friends. The impression created that day will stay with me forever: I realised how lucky Deirdre and I were to have three healthy little boys! Since that visit, I often wondered what I could do to help. A flash of inspiration arrived with the idea to make a collection of childhood memories of well-known Irish people for the children in the Hospital.

With six brothers and three sisters in our family, we constantly remind each other of our childhood. No one is allowed to forget their past, and as time goes on these memories become more treasured. Today we still get a great laugh from hearing these stories over and over again.

In general, Irish people show great curiosity about their heroes and heroines and while in most cases their adult lives have been well reported in the media, little is known about their childhood.

This book will end that curiosity and at the same time raise a few pounds for Crumlin.

Once Fin Breatnach gave the go-ahead for the book, I and my secretary Margaret with the help of other secretaries in the Oireachtas bunker drew up a list of well-known Irish personalities. We tried to strike a balance between different categories: Sport, Entertainment, Religion, Politics, Business — we wanted to cover the whole spectrum. With the names almost complete, we then had the job of finding addresses. In some cases we almost gave up, but with the help of friends, the necessary information was obtained. On 9 February 1995 the first batch of letters went out, asking people to put pen to paper and reveal a memory from their past.

Suddenly the book took on a new meaning for me, when a little friend Ciarain was killed. Immediately I got a fresh enthusiasm for the book. It was going to be published, it was going to be a success and it was going to be dedicated to Ciarain.

The replies began to roll in. There were some who preferred not to write and made a donation instead and there were others who for various reason were unable to contribute.

The response was wonderful, and as the memories began to arrive, Deirdre and I waited for the postman each day like children wait for Santa. We were not disappointed. The strangers were producing the goods and we felt very privileged to have so many famous people sharing their childhood memories with us.

Did you know that Albert Reynolds became a confirmed teetotaller after drinking a glass of poitín as a boy, followed by another glass of water to help him recover? Or that Garret FitzGerald's earliest memories are about hens? That Martin McGuinness nearly died when he was eleven, and that John Bruton's favourite subjects at school were history and geography? Or why Sinéad O'Connor likes silence? These were the kind of nuggets that arrived in the post each day.

One day we had Uncle Gaybo explaining why he turned out to be the 'thieving rascal and general no-good layabout which he is today'. The next day's post had Maureen Potter telling us how she became a teacher's pet with the help of her dead pet rat.

Stars of stage, screen, television journalism, literature, politics, business and sport responded to our call. Writers like James Plunkett, John B. Keane, Bryan MacMahon, Alice Taylor, Sam McAughtry, Ben Kiely, Roddy Doyle and poets Brendan Kennelly and Des Egan were proud to be numbered as contributors.

Amongst the world of business, Feargal Quinn told us how from the earliest of ages he learned the need for a back-up in case things went wrong, while the late Senator Gordon Wilson recalled that from invoices obtained in his father's drapery shop he was able to put an inspector from the Department of Education right about shoes and boots being manufactured in Killarney.

We also heard how the conqueror of Mount Everest, Dawson Stelfox, developed a taste for adventure picking blackberries in the Mourne Mountains. We laughed with Monica Carr as she recalled the first day the electricity was switched on in her parents' house, showing up dust that had been completely invisible until then.

Hurling maestro Eamonn Cregan told us with all sincerity why he doesn't laugh any more at anybody who claims to have heard the Banshee wailing, while Dr Noël Browne gave a very moving and graphic account of his close encounters with TB at the earliest of stages.

Great sporting days in Croke Park feature prominently, and for those who failed to make it to the big matches there are many memories of groups of neighbours—up to twenty at a time—huddled in kitchens listening to the magical radio commentaries of Michael O'Hehir in the days long before 'The Sunday Game'.

By the end of April sufficient stories had been received. Now I could go and talk to a publisher. While I had every confidence that I had the makings of a good book, confirmation from a professional was needed! So my first meeting with the publishers was very important, and thankfully Gill & Macmillan were quick to accept the idea. I was so happy. My dream was now going to be realised.

To all the contributors to this book, many, many thanks. To those who made a financial contribution, let me also thank you. Your donations are very much appreciated. I am indebted to the Buggy family for their inspiration and for bringing about my first visit to the Children's Cancer Hospital. I must thank Des Maguire, Breda Gleeson and

John Treacy for their invaluable advice and help.

To my secretary Margaret, my apologies for causing her so many headaches. She and her secretarial colleagues in the bunker showed total dedication in compiling the list. Míle Buíochas. To my wife Deirdre, I extend a special thanks for all her help and encouragement. Finally to my own parents, brothers and sisters, I owe the memory of my own childhood memories. Truly, 'Those were the Days'.

Seán Power
August 1995

GERRY ADAMS

Holy Flip Me Pink!

'**M**ake sure the driver doesn't go to sleep,' Uncle Paddy directed us again.

There were four of us in the back seat of the car. We stirred ourselves anxiously at the note of urgency in his voice. Dutifully we began to chant, for the umpteenth time. . . .

'Ten green bottles hanging on a wall,
Ten green bottles hanging on a wall.
And if one green bottle should accidentally fall,
There'd be nine green bottles hanging on the wall. . . .'

Uncle Paddy encouraged us, his voice rising in rhythm with ours.

'Louder,' he insisted. 'You can't be too careful. If the driver goes to sleep, we're all in trouble. How would youse like to be driving all this time? Youse would be hypnotised by now. Youse would be fast asleep. Louder! Holy flip me pink! Do youse want us to crash? Louder!'

Our Liam sang the loudest. He practically drowned out the rest of us. There was a nervous edge to his tone. We chanted noisily at him and our Paddy succumbed to almost choking, contagious laughter. He pounded the car seat with his fist and reduced the rest of us to a giddy, hysterical cackle.

Uncle Paddy's voice rose above the din. 'Nearly there now, lads. Don't give up! Holy flip me pink! What did that signpost say?'

'One mile,' our Seán shouted. Uncle Paddy led us in a new chorus.

'Only one mile more left to go
And I guess if we are lucky

1

We will end up in Kentucky
Only one mile left to go!'

Already the city-bound traffic was enveloping us in its flow. Uncle Frank, in the driver's seat, whistled happily along with us as he manoeuvred the McCauslands' hired car towards the city centre. A large green bus dwarfed our Morris Minor.

'Look at that!' said Uncle Paddy proudly. 'The widest street in Ireland! O'Connell Street. We're here, boys. Dirty Dublin!'

It didn't look too dirty to us. But it was crowded and the colours of the All-Ireland teams were already much in evidence as rival fans weaved their way along the thronged pavements.

'Didn't they do great?' Uncle Paddy asked Uncle Frank.

'I don't know what I'd have done without them,' Frank replied. 'I get awful sleepy on a long journey.'

Uncle Frank parked in a side street. Turning to us, he rubbed his eyes slowly with the heels of his hands.

'Getting back is the problem,' he said worriedly.

'No problem,' Uncle Paddy interjected. 'We'll keep you awake. Right, lads?'

'Right,' we assured him.

'Now. Who's hungry? Let's go.'

We ate in an Italian café across from the GPO. Afterwards we scampered skywards up the stairs to the top of Nelson's Pillar. Our uncles raised us shoulder high, for disappointingly, a wire restricted our view of the cityscape.

'Holy flip me pink!' we heard Uncle Paddy mutter. 'Wouldn't you wonder that they haven't taken old Nelson down?'

We went to a pub. Our Liam sang a song and got sixpence from one of the customers. We had orangeade and crisps. Our Seán and Liam drank some of Uncle Frank's Guinness. They let on they were drunk. Me and our Paddy couldn't drink 'cos we had made our Confirmation but we knew they weren't drunk. We had tried it before at Gerard Begley's wedding.

We slept that night in our cousins' house. It was great. Croke Park was brilliant the next day. We nearly lost our Liam.

On the way back to Belfast, we sang all the way. . .

'The cup's going over the border! The border, the border, the border! The cup's going over the border, and so say all of us!'

Our Liam and our Seán fell asleep at Banbridge. But me and our Paddy stayed awake the whole way.

BERTIE AHERN

I have many wonderful childhood memories, some sad, some happy. But the nicest I have, which regularly returns to mind, is that of a Sunday trip to Poolaphuca in the summer of '61.

It was around the second or third week in September, I remember, because we were back in school and all the talk was about Dublin being beaten by Wexford in the All-Ireland hurling by just a single point. I think the score was sixteen points to fifteen, or somewhere around that.

Another reason I remember that summer was because Cliff Richard's new song, 'A girl like you', was all the rage and I sort of noticed it, out of the corner of my eye!

The day was golden as we sped out in the bus past Tallaght village. Everybody on the bus was in great humour. My father was a great conversationalist and in the space of ten or fifteen minutes, he knew everybody in the nearest six or seven seats.

When we arrived in Poolaphuca, it was off with the clothes and into the togs while my father filled up his pipe and went for a stroll with two other men, a sacristan from

Santry and a milkman from Finglas. This suited my father down to the ground because he was somewhat of an expert on both topics, being farm manager to All Hallows College. The reason I remember both vocations is that Dad often spoke of this most pleasant conversation. In fact, one of the memorable features of the day was that everybody seemed to remember it and speak of 'that day out in Poola'.

After a dip in the icy water — even though the sun was high and hot — I lay back on the towel and relaxed for a few minutes, exulting in that after-swim glow that transfuses the body with incredible lightness. I heard a pounding of hooves and shouting nearby and quickly got my shorts, sandals and top on. It was a crowd from Inchicore. Their daddies worked in the railway sheds, and one of them had a real leather football, the big brown leather one with the white laces. This was one of the most coveted possessions any boy in my circle could have and here was a great opportunity to play real football.

After the 'G'is a game' was responded to with 'Alri', we proceeded to play three games of Gaelic, soccer and touch rugby. There was a blondie Inchicorian called Mugser who played on my team each time. He was an absolute flier and we played brilliantly together. I even scored in the Gaelic in spite of the fact that I normally played in the backs.

After the games, Mugser came down with me where my mam had laid out a lovely picnic of cheese and ham sandwiches, Mikado biscuits and glasses of red lemonade. Never did food taste so sweet, never did limbs pulse so proudly, never did the sun shine so sweetly. I will always treasure those golden moments. It is my favourite childhood memory.

DARINA ALLEN

I have always felt blessed to have had a charmed country village childhood. The eldest of nine children, I was brought up in a tiny village called Cullohill in Co. Laois. Every morning, I ran down the hill to the local school which in the winter was heated with big turf fires.

We were children of the village, part of a close rural community that cherished its young and rallied to help each other during the busier times of the farming year. Hay-making and threshing were the most exciting times for us. The minute school was over, we'd race over to Bill Walsh's farm, fling our satchels in the ditch and go to help with tossing the hay or stacking the sheaves of corn into stooks at first and then into hay stacks. We knew every process and watched the weather anxiously every afternoon as we sat at our desks.

Even at an early age, I gravitated towards the kitchen. I loved to watch Mary Walsh making the currant bread. I helped to peel the apples or chop the rhubarb for an apple cake or rhubarb tart for the men's tea, both special treats during these busy times.

During hay-making and threshing, sweetened tea was brought out into the fields in covered gallons or whiskey bottles wrapped in newspaper to keep the tea hot. Warm currant bread, called Spotted Dog, was cut into thick slices and buttered. We'd get a tremendous welcome when we appeared with the tea. Work would stop and the men would sit with their backs to a hay cock or stack of corn and relish the thirst-quenching tea.

Every evening the cows had to be milked. We weren't farmers but we did have a 'house cow' — a wicked black Kerry which had to be chased around the field every evening. Bill Walsh's cows were more obedient and lumbered home every evening from the pasture into the self-same stall in the cowshed.

No milking machines then, so occasionally I would help with the milking, sitting myself on a three-legged stool beside one of the docile cows which was guaranteed not to kick the bucket. Those were the days when one knew the personality of each cow. At the end of the milking, one dipped one's thumb in the milk and made the sign of the cross on the cow's side as a blessing.

Other highlights of the year were school holidays when I would pack my summer dresses and shorts into an old leather suitcase and take the bus to the Turnpike in Co. Tipperary. I spent the next few weeks on my grand-uncle's farm, helping to save turf, making butter and watching in deep fascination as my great-aunt made bread in the bastible and boxty on the griddle over the open fire. I searched in the ditches and all around the haggard and in the hay for nests. Occasionally, a hen or duck more canny than the others would arrive in from her secret hatching place with a clutch of chicks or ducklings which would enchant us for weeks.

On Sundays, we dressed up and went to Mass in the little chapel in Two-Mile-Borris. There was a bar of chocolate and maybe a packet of pastilles as a treat in John Maguire's shop or maybe a glass of lemonade in the snug of Cathy Corcoran's pub.

Every evening after the nine o'clock news, my grand-uncle would call for the prayers. We all knelt down around the open fire and took turns to recite the decades of the rosary and the 'Hail, Holy Queen' — another time, another world — happy, happy memories which I will cherish all my life.

CHARLIE BIRD

I was a child of the fifties and sixties. Born the same year as Prince Charles. Winkle-picker shoes, tight trousers, Brylcream and Elvis 'The Pelvis' Presley were, for me, 'the order of the day'. We also brought a penny into school every so often, for the black babies in Africa.

I grew up in the quiet middle-class suburb of Goatstown on the south side of Dublin. New housing estates were being built everywhere. It was the boom of the Lemass era.

It was a time of innocence, as well as a fear that the Russian bear was going to fire an atom bomb at America and we were all going to fry in a dark mushroom cloud.

The Russians, whom we were taught not to like, launched the first 'Sputnik' into space. I can vividly recall looking up in the sky early in the mornings or in the late afternoon for the small, bright object which we were told was a satellite. Maybe there were, after all, little green people on the moon, and some day they were going to find them.

Not many people in the neighbourhood had a television set. Those who had were easy to spot. A huge aerial sitting on the roof of the house announced its arrival. Occasionally we'd be invited into a neighbour's house to watch the Lone Ranger, his friend Tonto and his horse Silver. It gave a whole new dimension to our games of Cowboys and Indians.

Our summer holidays were spent playing football and fighting with the gang at the bottom of the hill. As we grew older, our games became more adventurous. Playing shop gave way to the more exciting 'spin-the-bottle'. The same two or three fellas always got to kiss the girls. I was not so lucky.

Even then, it was always greener on the far side of the street.

The local Stella Cinema in Mount Merrion gave us many pleasurable Sunday afternoons. This is where the real tingling of first love emerged. The groups of boys and girls arrived separately and sat separately as the big oyster shell opened its wide mouth to herald the start of another afternoon of adolescent fun. By the time we left the cinema with our eyes blinking to meet the dying sunlight, the make-up of the gangs had changed somewhat. A mysterious happening. There they were, fellows and girls, arm and arm together. What a strange expression it was — did so-and-so get off with what's-her-name?

I can remember the Cuban Missile Crisis and where I was the day John F. Kennedy was assassinated. These were the events which troubled our young and impressionable minds.

Like many children, I thought the world was coming to an end in those October and November days leading up to the blockade of Cuba. We prayed in the local national school in Dundrum that President Kennedy would save the world from a man called Nikita Khrushchev.

A year later, and our world was turned upside down once again. In the afternoons after school, I delivered shoes for the local cobbler, Jack O'Donnell. I can remember the afternoon well. I was cycling down the Drummartin Road with a bag full of shoes over the handle bars, when a woman came out of a house and told me that someone had shot President Kennedy in Dallas. Clearly she felt she had to tell someone this grave news. It was information which was difficult for me to come to terms with. I turned my bike around and headed back for the shoe shop, for fear the world was about to come to an end. This was a troublesome burden for a young lad to carry on his own.

Just two years earlier, as a ten-year-old, I had caught a glimpse of the great man himself as his fancy American car made its way around College Green in Dublin. I can't recall if I was waving the Tricolour or the Stars and Stripes. But sure as hell I was there. John F. Kennedy was everywhere you went in those days. At practically every door I went to delivering shoes, he looked out at me, pictured alongside Pope John Paul XXIII and Padraig Pearse.

Years later, my travels as an RTE journalist brought me to Washington and to Arlington National Cemetery where John F. Kennedy is buried. Many things have happened in the intervening years to blur not only my memory of JFK but also, to some extent, his image. Perhaps I now know that he was human. But standing by his grave, one still felt a sense of history.

It's certainly a long way from Goatstown to Washington.

FATHER HARRY BOHAN

Great Expectations

When I was growing up in the forties, my world was very small. But I didn't think so. To me, it was big, full and wonderful. It centred on a small village and a few miles each side of it. Because of that, every person, animal, tree, bush, field, house and road was a well-known and vital landmark. They were part of my growing up. They were part of us. They *were* us. I noticed when anything happened to any one of them.

So when Peig, Paddy's grey mare, was expecting a foal, I was excited. Paddy was our neighbour. Nellie was the woman of the house. They were like a father and mother to me. I spent most of my young life with them. Nellie is still with us, thank God. Peig and Jenny were the two mares and I loved them.

One Sunday morning after first Mass, Paddy called to our house. Martin, the workman, was with him.

'We are going down to the farm,' Paddy said to me.

I was delighted and excited because I felt that this could

be the day when Peig had her foal — a new presence. I longed to see what that presence would look like. I was looking forward to the days, weeks and months ahead, seeing Peig and her foal in the field at the back of the house. Peig would do most, if not all, of the rearing but we would be there too.

We walked to the farm, where Peig was. It was exactly one mile from the house. It was a beautiful, sunny Sunday morning — the kind of morning which was very special to us then. I would have associated Christ's resurrection with a morning like this, but that kind of morning was special then for less theological reasons. It was the morning for our best clothes. It was also the morning we all went to Mass, when people from the valleys and hills around came to bend the knee and bow the head. For many, the best clothes got an airing only on Sunday mornings. There were other 'airings' too. Bits of news were exchanged after Mass as the men congregated in groups outside the church. The weather, the price of cattle, the crops were discussed and, of course, the match. The women went off to the local shops.

That was the kind of morning Paddy, Martin and myself went to see Peig. When we got to the field, Peig was standing over her foal but *it was dead*. My happiness and expectancy turned to deep sadness. The sun continued to shine but a kind of darkness came over my young life. I was sad for myself but I sensed that this was nothing compared to Peig's loss. I don't remember how Paddy and Martin felt, but no farmer then or now likes to lose an animal and Paddy loved his horses.

We spent some time there and then Paddy put me on Peig's back. I was only eight and wouldn't have weighed heavily on her. It was my sad task to take her home. The first few hundred yards were difficult. She did everything to turn back. She didn't want to leave her baby. We eventually got her home.

That experience and that morning have never left my mind. In recalling it now, I hope I am underlining a way of life which centred around neighbourhood and neighbours, one in which we depended not only on one another but also on our animals. They were all special and we knew them — people, horses and cows — by name. We were part of one another. Times have changed since then.

It is interesting, however, that after years of depending on great entities, like the state and big organisations, there is a move to return to neighbourhood and family. People are at last beginning to realise that no human invention is more important than God's creation. My wish is that events of recent years will once again convince us in Ireland to think about returning to our neighbours, to a respect for one another and for the 'Peigs' of this world.

JACK BOOTHMAN

My boyhood memories all centre around farm events and GAA matches. Going to the village forge with my father, watching the horses being shod, listening to the men as they traded information and lies in equal parts, the smell of scorching hoof, the hiss of steam as the new hot shoe was thrown into the trough of water for tempering. All of these memories are still vivid today. I can still feel the pride of the day I was allowed to bring the horses on my own, riding one and leading two more. These weren't your average lightweight hunters, but massive sixteen-hands plough horses, each weighing in at sixteen hundred-weight.

The most vivid memory I have is going to a football match in Donard in the forties. Our mode of transport was, as always, a milk float in which we sat back-to-back. On this occasion, Blessington was playing Baltinglass and everybody was looking forward to a great contest, and hopefully, a 'bit of a mill'.

We set sail for Donard on Sunday after early lunch, with a frisky black mare, half trained, in the shafts. The 'Bossman' drove. I sat beside him, with Ned Carroll on my other side. My brother Mac sat in the back with an old man, Jimmy Quinn.

Our trip to Donard, eleven miles, was uneventful. We stabled the mare in Toomey's yard and went to the field. The old field in Donard was known as the 'Bawn' and had a hill along one side-line, almost like Clones. With no fencing, taking a side-line kick was fraught with possibilities.

The match was close and enjoyable, with the usual few interruptions, involving everyone. Unusually, a number of gardai was present, carrying blackthorn sticks. I can remember my father getting involved with them because he objected to them (a) interfering in what was basically a private shindig, and (b) using the blackthorns carelessly.

However, force of numbers settled that particular argument, the match ended and we set off for home. Coming up the street of Donard, who should step out but the sergeant who had been present in the Bawn a few minutes earlier.

Another argument ensued, which eventually descended into whether our method of transport was a trap or a cart. The subtlety of this argument was this: carts were obliged by law to have the name and address of the owner on a plate on the side, a requirement which was not extended to traps. The argument finished with the parting shot, 'You can stick your summons' etc. etc.

So we left Donard in great spirits. We had defeated the ancient rivals (twice), we had defended our honesty and our integrity against the forces of the Free State, and we had a high-stepping mare to take us home. However, fate had not finished with us yet.

When you come into the main Baltinglass/Blessington Road at Anneleckey Cross, there is a bog along the left-hand side which stretches up to Allens' farmhouse. We were dinging up the road home, with the frisky mare knocking sparks out of the metal, when suddenly, around a corner, came a man in a motorised wheel-chair. This wasn't one of your modern electric jobs, but one powered by a noisy two-stroke engine. Of course, the mare started to dance side-ways. But the 'Bossman', with a considerable amount of skill and also using a peculiar soft whistling sound, managed to keep the mare from going forward.

Everything would have been OK, but the driver of the wheel-chair, out of concern, stopped and held out his hand to the mare. That was it. Without a sound, she wheeled for the bog. My father let her at it, and she cleared the towpath and a thorn ditch, breaking a strand of barbed wire with her chest, and landed twenty feet out in Medcalf's bog. The only mishap was that Jimmy Quinn fell out of the back of the float with the fright. As he had been sitting facing backwards, he had been unaware of the drama unfolding.

Nothing was broken, on man, horse or harness. We trotted to the nearest gate and set off for home none the worse for our adventure. I was eleven when this episode occurred and to this day, it still sticks out in my memory.

Incidentally, the summons never arrived. Sergeant Bohan in Blessington calmed things down.

You will never get such excitement these days. A traffic jam in Carrick, Clones or Cork is all we have to look forward to now.

GILLIAN BOWLER

One of the good things about getting old has to be the fact that one can remember incidents in childhood with renewed clarity, if not hilarity. Not that getting old is really that bad. Like everything else in life, it has its good points, not least being that maturity brings a certain sense of security and a feeling that one has at last found a niche.

I often think that I have been one of the lucky ones as I can look back on my childhood days with a great fondness. Although I had what I now know to have been a fairly unusual adolescence, in that I spent a lot of it in hospital, this of course meant that I was essentially spoiled and I naturally revelled in every moment of it! I suppose I gave my parents a hard enough time because they must have worried and fretted about my health quite a lot, while I simply enjoyed the undivided attention and read voraciously and with unabandoned catholic taste.

My best childhood memories, however, go back decidedly further and a particular incident will always stay with me, and with my father, who was the unwitting and not entirely amused recipient! Although I must have been extremely young (and this is borne out by my perch on a high chair), I recall so clearly my father fussing over me and possibly trying to feed me at the time. But somehow, I managed to have a hammer in my hand, and to this day I know not how or why, but I struck! Perhaps the lure of his balding, egg-shaped head was too enticing to resist, but my doting Papa got the full brunt of my baby strength as I whacked him roundly and soundly on his very vulnerable pate! In an effort to exonerate my dreadful action, I convince myself today that I was sure he was a monster chocolate Easter egg specially proffered to me as a bribe or a treat for being good, but I have to admit that this stretches even my own credibility to its outer limits.

The upshot of this unexplained and uncompromising act of violence was that absolute mayhem ensued in our normally tranquil kitchen. My mother screeched uncharacteristically (a more placid individual one would travel far to meet), the china teapot went crashing onto the tiled floor, spewing its golden liquid content, and my father roared. Loudly. I inevitably joined in the fray and screamed at the top of my lungs. I remember feeling frightened and exhilarated all at once, but throughout, I was definitely aware of having been the cause of this disturbance.

I do not recall the resulting ambulance dragging my father off to have his gaping wound stitched. Nor do I clearly remember my mother's chalk-white face as she stared blankly at me, nor even how normality was eventually restored. However, the story has been enjoyed and savoured and recounted with great gusto over the years, perversely at the precise times when I have been trying to impress a fourteen-year-old suitor or precociously acting as the grown-up. The chaotic scene is still a source of embarrassment, richly relished by my family, unwilling to permit me to forget. Gentle oblivion would be my preference, but, as Dad points to his head, I have left my indelible mark!

NOËL BROWNE

'Your money or your life'

With the poet Philip Larkin, I agree that parents, 'Mum and Dad', can inflict deep and damaging scars on our childhood psyche. With safe fertility control now, for 'Mum and Dad', unasked, to confer life on the infant is questionable enough; needlessly to wound it, unforgivable. Our primal foetal cry is surely one of anguish at being born, and why not?

With myself, alas, it was my parents' early, needless deaths and a sense of loss with those of siblings, for which they could not be blamed, that scarred my persona with an always impending nemesis like a sense of foreboding and death.

Childhood in the twenties in Ireland was a time of civil war and death in the streets, as well as needless suffering, sickness and death in the homes for the peasant poor. The shock of a midnight ambush, just under our bedroom window, the last moments and the strident, pleading voice of a young soldier begging to live, shot down in the street below by brother Irish, mercilessly. Morning after, rough red-edged blood-soaked dirty-black potato sack, fig leaf, to cover the shame of his cowardly killing. My young consumptive father, terminally ill, pre-mortal attempts to rise himself and reassure us, 'Joe Browne is not going to die,' as he lay dying, and died. Later to die, my young mother, also a consumptive, four sisters and only brother, their children.

To memory, a winter's night and seven years of age, suddenly awake in dream or nightmare, in search of my mother. Sleep bewildered, barefoot, on cold linoleum, at the half-open door to her bedroom. As was the way then, credulous young Roman Catholic wife and mother of five already, in recent weeks helped by neighbour, strong and buxom Mrs Bracken, my mother had given birth to our latest, weeks-old sister, Marie Therese, willed by 'Almighty God and his Holy Mother', and obediently welcomed.

Hush, hush, as childbirth was always then in our simple peasant culture. Unexplained, a heap of blood-soaked cotton wool awaiting disposal.

Babies? 'They came from God mysteriously', 'down the chimney', 'found under a cabbage', 'a stork brought her', 'an angel brought her'. No doubt there would be an angel to take her back again to join the 'reject stock' of thousands of little angels born, needlessly sick, tormented and painfully dead, in our Republic.

Strangely, Marie Therese was not in bed with my exhausted, heavily-sleeping mother. Instead, in the wispy, shadowy indistinction of the night, under the window, a square box-like roofless structure. Out, from inside, a purple-violet glow threw patterns on the ceiling. A soft, sighing, whispering sound, overlaid by a minimally harsher, spasmodic bubbling, gasping sound of an infant's troubled breathing. At seven, tall enough to look over the tight safety-pinned Odlums flour-sack cotton walls of the square, in turn supported and framed by the sides of Marie Therese's infant cot. Mild surprise at the unprotected flame under a small thick flat-bottomed straight-sided tinker's kettle, its short straight spout, a funnel stuck in its mouth. White smoke teams 'the whispering sound' generated by the soft, steady, velvety-purple flame of the methylated spirits lamp under it. Pillowed in the shadowy depths, an apple-sized head of the tormented infant, twisting and turning, uselessly fighting for life-supporting air that wouldn't come. Wildly suckling in the warm, moist steam-filled mixture, generated by the tin-kettle steam engine, her fate already decided, she fought out her hopelessly one-sided struggle with death.

Our impoverished parents lovingly, futilely and, above all, prayerfully, compelled to devise their own home-made infant's intensive care unit. No doubt Mrs Bracken, untrained midwife, was its architect; my weary and heartbroken mother herself, as was my father, so soon to follow their infant daughter in death, its builder's labourer. Like the tigress, such mothers fight to save the lives of their newest new-born, dearly-loved little ones. No money, no doctor, no skilled nurse, no hospital; the highwayman Dick Turpin's principle of Irish medical practice — 'Your money or your life.'

Slowly and painfully, Marie Therese suffocated by the spreading broncho-pneumonic tuberculosis as it strangled her pencil-slim tiny throat. Newly born, newly dead. Small white coffin-shaped box, for the minuscule remains to be buried in the consecrated, cold grey clay of Cornamagh. 'She's with the angels in heaven', no doubt, with my mother, my father, brother and sisters, as with thousands of others, too poor to pay the high price a life can cost among the Irish.

Surely the most rewarding days of my life were when, unexpectedly and wonderfully as Minister for Health in 1948, I was empowered by the people to spend, all over the

Republic, the equivalent of four to five hundred million pounds, building hospitals for our Marie Thereses of all ages and sexes; hospitals, an international jury later adjudged to be, with peerless Sweden, 'the finest hospitals in the world'. One of these was our magnificent Crumlin Children's Hospital in Dublin.

In the Department of Health, we wanted to go on, to give all our mothers and their children the right to free medical care whenever they needed it, in every one of our fine new superbly equipped and staffed hospitals. Alas, our Catholic bishops pronounced it to be a mortal sin, and would not allow it. All my colleagues in government obeyed the bishops, and abolished the scheme. I did not, would not and could not agree that to look after the sick, especially our mothers and their children, could be wrong.

JOHN BRUTON

My father, who is still active at eighty-six, is a farmer. So I spent a lot of time following him around as he organised things on the farm. My most graphic memory is of hay-making, putting the hay up into cocks, and later bringing it into the barn on the bogey. The summers were always sunny then!

I was at primary school in Cabra in Dublin. I remember the boys in the school — it was an all-boys school — organising ourselves into rival armies for playground battles. The two groups lined up in military formation and charged at one another when the order was given. I am sure young people today are not as militaristic.

I do not know when I first became aware of politics, but I do remember arguments in school about the elections of 1954 and 1957. I first got interested in politics through school debates after I went to secondary school in 1959.

At school, my favourite subjects were history and geography. I am afraid I always felt that I was hopeless at mathematics, and it was only long afterwards, when I was forced to do mental arithmetic to work out what to charge people when doing a night's work as a barman, that I found out that I could do it quite well after all. After that, I came to the conclusion that people should not assume that they are bad at a subject without giving it a fair try!

As a child, I used to go to stay with different cousins of mine during the summer holidays. This was very interesting, as I got to see places I had only heard of before that. My cousins have remained among my closest friends since then.

My mother had a sister who was a nun in Holyhead in Wales. I remember going over on a mailboat to Holyhead at the age of four or five to visit my aunt. I also remember the terror I felt when I got lost in a shop in Holyhead for about three minutes — it seemed like an eternity at the time! My aunt, who had been a nun in occupied France during the war, died a few years afterwards in Holyhead.

I do not remember taking holidays as a child. I do remember going to the sea at Gormanstown. This was a very exciting excursion. I also remember attending the point-to-point races in Ratoath — a photograph still exists of a serious-looking little boy with a black beret standing in front of a happy group of relatives who had made a few bob.

The first time I visited the Continent was when I was seventeen and my parents took me on holiday to Brittany and Normandy. Since then, I have had an abiding interest in France and the French language. It is a different world from the Anglo-American one that we see all the time through our televisions and newspapers. It is, I think, very important for an Irish person to see the world from a different angle from time to time.

BISHOP JOHN BUCKLEY

Looking back now, the scene was enthralling, a rural patchwork quilt, a composite of swathes of beauty from around the world — a river scene from a Japanese brush painting, hills as interesting as the English Cheviots, glorious mountains from a Himalayan postcard, fertile patches intensely cultivated in Dutch style, and binding all together was the Scottish heather as it changed from purple to red to pink, with a timid white nosing through here and there.

The day was sunny — it was Confirmation day in my native village of Inchigeelagh, Co. Cork. What a crowd! Grandmothers and grandfathers looking young again. Aunts in their Sunday best, uncles smiling, mothers and fathers proud and happy that another spiritual hurdle had been taken. Children everywhere — like colourful butterflies, running, chatting, chewing, calling out to pals. There was a sense of complete joy and happiness in the very air. I could borrow a line from Wordsworth, and mean it: 'Bliss was it in that dawn to be alive, and to be young was very heaven'.

It was not my Confirmation day. An older brother was being confirmed, so I attended with my family. I will always remember that day for another reason, as it was my first encounter with the game of road bowling. I was six, but I now know that this noble, healthy sport is indigenous to Cork city and county.

After the Confirmation ceremony and formalities were over, a large number of those present moved outside the village. I went too, and must have been open-mouthed with anticipation. Some big boys took off their coats and caps and did a few physical jerks on the grassy border at the side of the road. Soon, the humming and chatting began to die down. Something was happening — and did it happen! I felt I was in a different world, and that I was part of something great.

Then, the mental study of lengths of road began; you could see the players talking to themselves, and their faces were different. It made me wonder. In a second, a loud cheer rent the air, then another, and another. Big iron bowls (twenty-eight ounces in weight) were being sent along the road at the speed of sound.

Suddenly there was a pause, and all looked around. The Bishop of Cork, Most Reverend Daniel Cohalan, who had performed the Confirmation ceremony, appeared in a motor car. Was he coming to referee? No, he was going to the parish house for his dinner. I remember not being sure of what to do, but I heard the bigger boys say, 'Should we kneel or run?' We hadn't time to do either because the car drove on.

What did the bishop think of the road-lined smiling faces? Did he think we were forming a guard of honour to greet him? *Níl fhios agam*, but we bowled on — without attempting to bowl him over! That was many years ago, and my love for road bowling as a sport goes back to that memorable day in Inchigeelagh.

I have enjoyed developing road bowling skills as a student, as a priest, and now as a bishop. It is a sport that is part of the texture of West Cork, a sport that is bred in our bones and entwined in our lives. It provides entertainment, builds community and brings people together. It is a great unifying bond in any area. It was one of the only forms of recreation in our younger days.

GAY BYRNE

This is one of the most hackneyed stories of juvenilia of all time, for it is told in stirring detail in my much-acclaimed book, *The Time of My Life*, and has oft been repeated, but here goes, anyway.

We lived in Rialto Street, off the South Circular Road, and I was in Rialto national school, now a community centre. I guess I was in 'high babies' or maybe in first class — I would have been about six or so and my teacher was Miss Sweeney, with whom I was madly in love. Apart from anything else, she had a terrific pair of legs, and I've retained my fondness for shapely female legs ever since, which just goes to show what a good educational grounding will do.

Monaghan's shop was on the corner of Rialto Street and of course I passed it every day on the way home. They had vegetables and fruit on display stands outside the shop and these were left unattended all day, for we lived in more honest times then. Or so they thought, until I came along. One of the days — and I cannot recall giving it much thought or pre-planning — I nicked an apple off the stand and walked on. No one saw me, and I relished munching it all the way home. Unfortunately, if you're going to be a successful bandit and major criminal, you have to keep your wits about you and remember where you are and who you're talking to. I was inexperienced, and went into the house with the butt of the apple (core, to you) still in my hand. My mother, a permanently deeply suspicious woman where all her sons were concerned, asked me where I'd got the apple. I fumbled, not to say mumbled, my reply and she was not satisfied. She pressed the matter, and under extreme cross-examination, I caved in and became a cringing, whinging wreck. I admitted my wrong-doing, made a full confession, followed by a firm purpose of amendment.

Wasn't enough for my ma.

A woman of the highest moral standards, she saw impending criminal tendencies staring her in the face. And nipping trouble in the bud was always part of her strategy. She donned her coat and took my little savings box with the slot in it, and marched me down to Monaghan's. It was a biggish shop for what it was, and there were a lot of people in it. To me, it looked like a department store with 10,000 in it. She stood in the centre of the shop and called for the attention of the proprietor, Mr Monaghan. She then announced that this person — little me — had taken an apple off the stand without payment, and she invited Mr Monaghan to take from my savings the appropriate amount. He took a knife to the slot and extracted one penny, which he reckoned would cover it.

She then requested me to apologise to one and all for my action and, not having much option, I complied, whinging all the while. The lesson having been learned, I then left with as much dignity as I could muster.

And that's how Uncle Gaybo turned out to be the thieving rascal and general no-good layabout which he is today.

I bet you often wondered.

DES CAHILL

I don't consider myself to have been a hooligan as a youngster, but there was one particular incident that might have got me into a lot of trouble.

Well, I suppose it *did* get me into trouble, but not as much as I deserved. I was about eleven or twelve at the time. It was a Sunday night and there were four or five of us hanging around the road. It was about 9.00 pm and darkness had just descended.

We were sitting on the wall, chatting about sport, I presume, and complaining about having nothing to do. (Nothing has changed with young teenagers!) I can't remember exactly who was with us, but I imagine it was Brian and Mark Keogh, Johnny Murphy and Oisin Troddyn.

Anyway, unlike the others, I had the burden of having

one of my little brothers with me, so we probably weren't talking about girls. Imagine the shame if Pat, who was then about eight years of age, went back to the house and told them I was talking about girls!

We were discussing what to do, but couldn't really think of anything. There wasn't much point in doing 'knick-knocks' (ringing a door bell and running away). By now every adult in the neighbourhood knew our hiding places. One of the lads then told us about the 'rope-trick'.

This is where you split the group up on the pavement on each side of the road. You line up, one behind the other, as if preparing for a tug-o'-war. You don't have a rope, of course, but as a car approaches, the group on each side pulls hard on the imaginary rope, the approaching driver slams on the brakes, and you all run away before he realises what's happening.

Anyway, as it was explained to us, we lined up and waited for a car. It was a pretty quiet road at the time, but after a few minutes we saw a car coming. We lined up and got ready to pull this imaginary rope.

Well, it worked a treat, as the driver skidded to a halt. I realised how dangerous it was, but being kids, we all cracked up laughing. However, for some reason, the driver didn't find it too funny. We could tell by the look on his face. So while he pulled himself together, the others all darted off to hide.

It was only then that the horror of the situation dawned on me. As I sprinted away (I was athletic in those days!), I heard the little pitter-patter of tiny feet behind me. No, not the driver, but my little brother, Pat.

Oh God! I knew he wouldn't be fast enough to run away from the driver, who was now getting out of the car. So I grabbed his hand and we ran around the corner. There was a bunch of fir trees around the walls of one of the houses in the *cul-de-sac* to Ashton Park, so I picked up Pat, threw him in between two of the trees, and hopped over the wall into the gap between the next two trees.

But as soon as I landed, I heard an almighty buzzing noise. I had thrown Pat into a nest of wasps! Pat started screaming, I started to panic, and the driver, who was now almost upon us, stopped dead in his tracks. He didn't know whether to come up and kill us or laugh at us.

He backed off. I dragged Pat home, where my mother spent the next hour getting wasps out of his hair and clothes, and I had to pay the consequences.

So much for little brothers!

NOELLE CAMPBELL-SHARP

Sugar 'n spice and all things nice,
That's what little girls are made of . . .

I was always extravagant. I wanted to save the shiny shilling I got for weeding the vegetable garden and other weekly chores, but Woolworth's shiny ice cream machine in Wexford's narrow Main Street steadily seduced this seven-year-old with promises of lusty licks and surreal sucks.

Her tongue wandered round and round the cool white cream, careful not to let a drop drop. And then she bit a bit off the bottom; so the remains of the creamy liquid could be sucked through before devouring, with smug satisfaction, the biscuit container of this Saturday morning delight!

I was always impatient too. Once, having discovered the way to town on my first day at school, and having found the little sweet shop on the outskirts of town, I put on my best skirt, stole my home-made and impregnable wooden money box and 'drove' my three-year-old foster-sister in her pram the three miles into 'the big smoke'.

There, having ordered a bag of bulls-eyes, sticky liquorice pipes with hot and hard red fireballs and romantic pastel lozenges along with two lucky bags, she plonked the wooden box of money up on the counter. The deal having been struck, the contract made and hasty sampling going on below, the resourceful shop assistant managed, with some dexterity and with the aid of an ivory-handled knife, to extract through the slot, sufficient coins to cover the purchase price.

I was always confused and astounded by adult fuss. She couldn't understand the foster-mother's fear, her rage, her rail, her fist; the concerned wails of women riding bikes saying, 'You'll catch it when you get home, Missie!' And, then strange news as the disappearance for seven hours of some two children, a five- and a three-year-old!

MONICA CARR

Naturally, brought up in the era of babies coming from under gooseberry bushes, I never enquired what weight I was at birth. I was always a *big* little girl, so probably my long-suffering mother was delivered of a ten-pounder, but that's beside the point, well and truly, today.

Reason I mention it is to explain how embarrassing it was being a cowardly, big child, born into a family that worshipped horses and dogs, and to a father who certainly had never heard of, leave alone read, Dr Spock.

The others took to jumping up on ponies (which were always around a farm in those pre-motor-car days) as a matter of course. Father, a good horseman in his younger days, gave us lessons or, more correctly, commands, on the lawn at home and the siblings galloped away across the long Dipping Tub field, like the wind.

When my turn came, I was given a most reluctant leg up, whimpering in terror as I clung on like a sack of potatoes. Father, disappointed, I suppose (with hindsight), at siring a child with a yellow streak, lost patience, lifted me down ungently, discharging the Parthian shot as he stalked off that I'd 'never be any b—— good anyway'.

Apart from such insensitivity, he was a kindly, good father, but that is certainly one of my earliest memories, plus the legacy it bequeathed of no interest whatever in racing.

Something else I often think about is the influence of pictures on small children.

Typical of the farmhouses of the day, our home was 'well-accoutered' with 'Stags at Eve', framed samplers worked by long-gone aunts, Grattan's Parliament and scores of hunting prints. One particular print hanging over the piano in the parlour, where the entire family sat every evening after tea in winter — fox, hounds, red-coated riders streaming across a hilly field — surely came, I always thought, from our own 'Six Acres' up the road from the hall door.

All the marble and grandeur of the Irish parliament picture was my childish idea of what heaven would look like, minus the knee-breeched politicians, of course.

Upstairs it was all religious pictures in the bedrooms and landings. Large memorial pictures of long-dead relations, soberly framed in black (for mourning), abounded there too. Death, come to think of it, is very much part of childhood memories and oddly not in any macabre way. Probably because we were lucky enough not to be touched by any immediate bereavement, but I recall attending wakes in the village during school lunch-times.

Quite a thrill it was, getting inside doors of houses normally closed to us. We all knew the rules exactly — no talking, down on your knees in the wake room, prayer for the departed, sprinkle holy water with a bit of palm or box, down the stairs, and out.

Lots of mourning dress worn then, I remember. Widows in black for years and men with black bands on their arms.

Mourning handkerchiefs too, deep black border for the first six months, decreasing in depth until the year was out.

The day the electricity was turned on is another vivid memory. The acute embarrassment on my mother's face when she saw how dusty everything was in the upper reaches of the big high-ceilinged kitchen. The utter wonder of light outside in the dark yard was something we constantly marvelled at, until we got used to it.

Quite a while before we invested in electrical gadgets, apart from the kettle. Food mixers, carving knives, blankets, even electric fires, seemed sinful extravagances, I recall.

Back further, I have a precious memory of the laburnum tree at the road-gate which had both pink and yellow blossoms. Enormously proud of that unusual tree we were. It grew tall over the wall behind which we had a marvellous 'Babby-house', entrance to which was effected by pulling back a lovely springy branch that slapped back, providing that wonderful secret privacy that children relish so much. The games we played there, setting up 'blue and white and speckled lore' — 'chainies' in actual fact — the bits of broken crockery which we hoarded like gold dust.

We spent hours making butter and cakes and pies out of mud and water, decorating them with flower petals. And there was our 'shop' too, in the corner of the 'trap-house' with smoothed-out tea and sugar bags, filled with sand and leaves, and when my father's back was turned, 'clarendo' — not sure of the spelling, but it was a maize mixture (not wildly unlike corn flakes) which was fed to the pigs — or was it the calves? Memory also plays tricks as we know, so I'll stick to what I'm sure of.

That right-of-way passed four fields to the village, down-hill all the way, so we ran, but trudging back, usually with laden message bags during the war years, was a different kettle of fish. Different in every season, of course, and we recognised every sign and change. The increase in the number of nests in the rookery, the position of the stepping stones at Guttery Gap, the bubbling swift-flowing little stream where on warm summer days we drank the best of spring water from our cupped hands and on other days fished for tadpoles.

I remember Easters when all the talk going to and from the church services was of 'sittin' hens and 'risin' hens, of fine or poor clutches of chickens, of whether your turkey-hen was ready for her annual visit to the Station Cock in the next parish. Taking same turkey-hen on that trip, strapped securely on the carrier of your bicycle, was a woeful embarrassment when you had to cycle through the village, and sure as eggs, the wretched bird would poke her head out of the concealing bag just as you passed the 'corner boys' — a signal for whistles and jeers.

Trips to Dublin on the train, the same train we always watched out for as we sat drinking the strong, sweet, sugared and milked brew in hay-fields of the thirties and forties. The evening train was always a signal for someone to go for the cows and I recall counting the number of luggage carriages — which gave us an indication of how the fair had gone in Tullow that day.

The pantomime at Christmas was an annual treat, staying as we did with grandparents in Stoneybatter. It was the pantomimes that gave us an indication of what songs were popular, and sheet music of same (for sixpence) was always bought before we left for home.

The lowing of cattle being driven up Prussia Street for the Dublin market, which we heard from our beds, was a homely sound in great, slightly frightening Dublin.

UNA CLAFFEY

Some of my earliest childhood memories involve Our Lady's Hospital in Crumlin. I grew up in Drimnagh near what was commonly referred to as 'the field', a large, open space which somebody, somewhere, probably thought of as a park or even intended would someday be a park. At the top of the field and bordering on the Crumlin Road was the site for the 'new children's hospital'. My sister, who is older than I, has vivid memories of the large granite wall which bordered the site. Some of that granite was to play a special part in a childhood event which I remember quite vividly.

In working-class Dublin in the fifties, few families had cars and the baby buggy hadn't been invented. So babies were taken out for walks, left to sun in front gardens kicking up their heels, in what seemed to be everlasting sunny days, in beautifully sprung high prams. Meanwhile, on the street, we played 'beds' in spring, kicking our 'piggies' of old shoe polish tins, skipping in the long summer evenings, and 'relievio' as winter drew in, when it was time to pour water on the roads on freezing nights to make slides. There were also, of course, marbles along the footpaths, 'snatch-the-bacon', cards and all the other street games we played in the pre-television age and still found time to read books!

As well as all this, I was the proud owner of a doll's pram, modelled on those beautiful babies' high prams, which was bequeathed to me by my sister. It even had a compartment under the seat for storage.

When I was about six, construction of the children's hospital finally got underway. The Dromard Road field became an extension of the site and a new source of adventure.

One day while playing there with my beautiful maroon-coloured doll's pram, I found some granite pieces. Knowing how my mother liked to put these 'stones' in her front garden, I loaded up the pram. How foolish I was, for behind the delight at my unsolicited gift was the horror on my mother's face when she looked at the pram. By the time I got to the bottom of Dromard Road, its springs had collapsed under the weight of the 'stones'. It was indeed a sorry sight.

There were several other visits to the hospital

throughout my childhood. After having my arm set in plaster following a fall on my new skates, my mother bought me my first Jacob's Club Milk. I can still remember my amazement at what to me then was a real treat — its dark brown wrapper, so much more sophisticated looking than today's brightly coloured one, then the foil, then the thick, thick chocolate. Even now I can remember sinking my teeth into it. There was the trip to get 'lifts' on the soles of my shoes so I wouldn't grow up with flat feet and a host of other visits to repair the damage of a rough-and-tumble but very happy childhood.

SEAN CLARKIN

Team-mates

The year was . . . Oh, never mind . . . the thing was, I was special. At least I felt so! I was a member of the panel that was to represent the school in a Leinster final! All round, in the dark, sparse spaces of school, I felt eyes were looking, minds saying, 'Yes, he is one of them!'

Though I wasn't a Boarder, during those last weeks I felt more completely part of the place. Day-boys like me were just a minority and suffered the fate of all minorities. We were isolated by the privilege of being able to escape the pervading smell of boiled cabbage every evening, no matter how Treblinka-ish the day had been. It was years later, and in different circumstances, that I realised that teachers too escape. Day-boys were also, envy of envies, fed adequately. Each morning, while the others were attended by their jailers, we were taken to where Day-boys seldom went. Here, at the source of those dreadful cabbage smells, we were dosed with raw eggs by an old-fashioned nun. An old-fashioned nun in those days was really something. Years later, I found out that they got the idea from a parent who raised greyhounds. During these preparations, the emphasis was very definitely on the physical.

This contrasted sharply with the other preparations which largely consisted of rosaries and rushed visits to the church before each exam. One particular student surprised us all by even going to Mass each day and then failing miserably. He was left bereft of even that excuse.

The contrast went unnoticed even though each area was ruled over by priests. The feeling was 'they must be right'. I can't help thinking that nobody noticed the fate of the unmarried mothers who ended up in Irishtown. We seldom saw the forbidding outline of the Good Shepherd Convent unless on the way to the graveyard. Sometimes at Christmas, however, the loneliest time of the year, I passed it, chewing a stolen turnip. One of my 'holly fields' lay thereabouts.

We question more nowadays. Why, for example, were 'unmarried' (reverend and childless!) Mothers held in such high esteem while 'unmarried mothers' were despised? It must, I suppose, have been clear then. It's not clear now.

When we did the Leaving Cert, about half of the team went away to join the black-and-white team. The ultimate ambition of some of these was to wear purple. None that I know joined that team. I joined the black-and-whites for a while. For a while more I felt special. Some say they don't feel special anymore.

Sometimes, even now, when I hear a member of the black-and-whites in the pulpit, I wonder that I could once have been a team-mate. Sometimes I even think it's time to sack the Manager. Sometimes in church, I imagine I hear Lambeg drums. An awful thought crosses my mind on these occasions — have I finally joined the Orange team?

PADDY COLE

My childhood memories would have to include happy summer days in Co. Monaghan when my father and I would fish for trout in the local rivers or go coarse fishing in the lakes. My late father, Paddy Cole Snr, was a great lover of wildlife and the outdoor life. He was a very patient man who could wait for hours until the time was right to fish a certain stretch of river. He taught me all the little tricks, to know where the fish were feeding, and the best time to fish.

He was a musician who also drove a mail van. He'd take the mail all around the sub post offices and then wait for four hours or so to collect the mail on the way back. These few hours were precious to us, as it was then we did our fishing.

We'd arrive in Cormeen Lane in Aughnamullen, to Mrs Susan Marron. There we'd have tea and home-made bread, hot off the skillet. The rods would be brought out and off we'd go. All the days seemed to be hot and sunny. These days we'd fish for perch or roach. On dull days we were after the trout. The trout to us was the king of all the fish. Harder to catch, and a great fighter! I remember catching a three-pound trout in Derrygoony River, and it took us ages to land it.

If the weather was bad, we stayed in Mrs Marron's. My father would take out an alto saxophone and we'd do an hour or so at the old Selmer tutor. I hated saxophone practice at that time.

I didn't go with him every day, as I'd have a summer job, but it made it all the sweeter when the day came around when I could go. I still do a bit of fishing, and if I was away with the band over the years in foreign countries and saw a good flowing river, I'd always get flash-backs to those days in my youth. I actually organised fishing trips with other musicians. When I was in Las Vegas, we went up the

Colorado River, past the famous Hoover Dam, and fished for trout. We also fished in Lake Mead. Over there they use things like cheese for bait. Not the fly or worm we use here. I remember telling my father we were using cheese as bait in Las Vegas. He laughed heartily, saying he wouldn't even take it to the river in a sandwich!

STEPHEN COLLINS

On a fine summer's evening in the middle of the 1960s, I stood on the banks of the little river that flowed through my grandfather's farm in Co. Longford, below the hill of Ardagh. I had been trying for days, without success, to catch a trout using a fishing rod with a length of line attached to the tip.

That was the way my grandfather had fished as a boy in the 1890s and he made me the kind of tackle he remembers from his own childhood. He showed me how to put a worm on the hook and let the current carry the bait into the deep pools which were likely to harbour a trout.

My father showed me how to fish for trout in this river, and his father showed him, and his father before that, all the way back since our family first came into this country. 'You are the last one who will ever fish the Graffogue River like this,' he told me.

I spent so may fruitless days that granddad began to believe that there were no trout left in the river. I was convinced there were because I had seen the ripples as they rose for flies in the evening. Even though I couldn't catch one, I knew they were there.

I also felt a violent tug on the line from time to time and when I pulled it out, the worm was half gone. Pinkeens, or leebeens as we called them, also nibbled at the bait but the strength of the bites showed that something much larger was lurking there somewhere.

One evening, as the sun was sinking slowly in the north-west and clouds of flies hovered above the river, the bait was taken so firmly that I knew I had to have a fish on the line. I waited for an age until I was sure it couldn't escape before hoisting the rod and lifting a wriggling trout clear of the river.

I still recall the amazement I felt at the beauty of the fish. It had exquisite red spots along its silvery sides and there was a dramatic contrast between its black back and its white belly. I felt like putting the panting creature back in the water but I couldn't get the hook out of the trout's mouth. I rushed across the fields to the house and burst into the kitchen with the fish still on the line.

After granddad had expressed his delight at my catch and the fact that there were still trout in the river, I told him that if he could get the hook out, I would put the fish back.

'Indeed and you will not,' he replied. 'He is big enough to eat.'

My grandmother put the pan on the range as granddad showed me how to clean out the fish. He then slid the supple trout into the heavy black frying pan where it sizzled in granny's home-made butter.

As it cooked, the fish's white flesh gave off a mouth-watering aroma. When it was done, we divided it into three small portions. It was the tastiest meal of my life.

SISTER M. CONSILIO

First Steps

I remember my father's footsteps. His feet seemed huge when he stood me up on them, supported me with his hands and shuffled me along with small steps that I could manage. The game was fun, and I felt his support, unfailing then, as always afterwards.

I was three then, and it is one of many memories that are still vivid after half a century.

There was the day when strangers were working in the house. The usual order was upset. Jumping suddenly from the fireside bench, I knocked over the kettle that stood in the hearth and was badly scalded. My six-year-old sister, Agnes, was angry with the nurse who came to dress the burns because of the pain she was causing her little sister. But that event taught me something of the pain involved in healing. I knew that the nurse was my friend.

Agnes was co-conspirator in many of my enterprises when I was a three-year-old. Between us, once on a winter's day, we decided to clear up the muddy cow tracks in a field using a brush and a shovel. Before long, we were both up to our eyes in mud and were trying to wash ourselves down in the freezing pond when mother arrived to the rescue. She soon had us warm and dry. It was not the last time that tasks turned out to be more than they had first appeared!

That was the year for me to start school. Coming home one day, I saw that my new doll, a recent present, was missing from its special place in the window and was nowhere to be found. The mystery was solved when my mother gently explained that it had been given to a girl who had none. Possessions were to be shared, and as a small child, I saw that this was how my parents lived.

The highlight of the school day at age three was coming home through the fields in the evening with my head tucked under the tail of Joe's coat. When my little wellingtons got too tight, it was Mossie who helped pull them off, warning that my leg might come too. My father gave the boys — Mossie, Joe and Johnny — a calf each. When Johnny sold his, I was made privy to the secret of the year — the money was hidden in a cocoa canister under the thatched roof of the stable. Johnny lifted me up to view the can and said, 'Any time you want anything, you can go to that canister.' He was actually saying, 'Anything I have, you are welcome to it,' and that has been the story ever since.

It was not so with everyone. I remember the boys who

'mended' my sweet bag for me — and gave it back full of waste paper, the sweets gone. And the man who mocked me and wounded my feelings because I lisped. Worst of all was Mollie, who paid me for the hard work she had set me — with one solitary sweet — and kept the whole bag to herself. Few adults know how important these things are to a child of three.

These little incidents were just a glimpse of the fear and cruelty outside, a faint preview of the world of pain and war and turmoil, far from my beautiful countryside home and its carefree, happy days.

Although the individual events are so clear to me, even more vivid is the overall memory of the happiness of my family life. Luxuries were few and we all worked hard, but our house was always full of laughter and fun and love and faith, and kindness for family, friends and strangers alike. I feel a surge of warmth when I remember it, and thankfulness for all that was given to me then.

When I grew up, I trained as a nurse and afterwards became a nun. My name became Sister Consilio. Nowadays, at Cuan Mhuire, I work to help those who are hurt and vulnerable, whose memories and experiences have been so very different from my own. With love and shelter and support, they too can take the early steps towards healing and happiness.

LOUIS COPELAND

I idolised the Beatles as a young lad. I was in St Patrick's national school in Drumcondra when they were in Dublin on tour, appearing in the Adelphi Cinema. The word got out that George Harrison had a cousin living in Clonturk Park in Drumcondra, the route that I took to walk home every day, and that he would be paying a visit to his relations.

I remember leaving school to go home for my dinner. On the way back to school, I decided to wait around George Harrison's cousins' house to see if I could see him. I was due back in school at two o'clock. I waited until two o'clock. No sign of him. I said to myself, I'll wait another half an hour.

I walked up and down the road outside the house. No sign of him. Three o'clock came and went. In the end, I waited until seven o'clock and at that stage I decided to give up and go home. It was a great disappointment to me, as I had not seen George Harrison, and to make matters worse, I was not too popular.

I learned that George Harrison went to see his cousins the following day.

The memory will always stick in my mind.

EAMONN CREGAN

Limerick city in the early to the mid fifties was a lovely town to grow up in. It was not too small and it certainly was not too big.

It had, and still has, many fine features. O'Connell Street was one of the finest in the country, with its beautiful Georgian houses. The city boasted six picture houses and I do not know how many churches, although there were a fair share, especially the Redemptorists or 'the Fathers' as we knew it, where seven-to-twelve-year-olds used to go on Friday nights to the confraternity. Boy, we dare not miss a Friday or the priest would want to know where we were. The Tantum Ergo was sung with great fervour.

There was the 'Bomber Field' where we played soccer and hurling. Soccer, wasn't that a foreign game? The

People's Park, where young fellas could actually play games, unlike today.

Anybody who wanted to swim went to the Corbally Baths. You either sank or swam. I sank below the water. The schools in our area were the Model School, Leamy's or St Brendan's as it is known today, Sextons, the Crescent, Laurel Hill and the Mount.

In the early fifties, our family was sitting down to breakfast one morning in the dining room of Hanratty's Hotel. At the table were Daddy and Mammy (Ned and Hannie to their friends), Micky (latter-day name Michael) and Pudsey (or Conor as he is known today). The reason we were having breakfast in Hanratty's Hotel is because my mother owned it.

Suddenly my big sister Noreen burst into the room, her eyes bulging with fright. What was wrong now, we wondered. She then asked, in a high, squeaky voice, 'Did anyone hear the noise on the street at about 2.00 am this morning?'

None of us had and we just laughed at her. Micky and I were delighted she was caught out. Two days later, a woman living across the road from us died. That was the first time we had ever heard of the Banshee. To this day, we (Micky and I) do not laugh at anyone who has heard the Banshee. A week after the Banshee incident, something happened out at sea. A ship was sinking in the Atlantic and tremendous efforts were made to save the crew and the ship. As far as I can remember, this went on for at least four days and it was on radio and in the *Evening Press*. I forget the name of the ship but I do remember the name of the captain. He was Captain Carlson and the amazing thing was, he made sure his crew were safe and rescued and then, when it was time for Captain Carlson to leave his ship, he declined. He was going to try and save the vessel.

We were enthralled by the courage of this man who might be drowned.

After many days, his ship was eventually towed to land

and if my memory served me correctly, he was met by the mayor of Limerick, Steve Coughlan, when he arrived at Limerick docks to a tumultuous reception.

These, then, were some flashbacks to the Limerick of my youth.

As the song says, 'Limerick is beautiful as everybody knows.' Limerick, despite its wants, has always been beautiful to me and the memories of it remain etched in my mind.

PADDY CULLEN

I would class myself as an inner-city boy — sorry, person — one cannot be too careful! Name dropping, I lived across the road from the Sheridan family, who now have a famous son called Jim, or 'Shamie', as he is known to us. Now he has films like *My Left Foot* and *In the Name of the Father* to his string of credits, not to mention that fabulous stage production of *The Risen People* done with his brother Peter.

The Sheridans had the first TV in Seville Place and I was one of the many young boys and girls who sat in their house and watched it because their door was always open.

The funeral of 'Da' Sheridan was an experience never to be forgotten. Sad and glad were stirred together as I walked shoulder to shoulder with Daniel Day-Lewis through Glasnevin cemetery to Da's final resting place.

I was a member of O'Connell Boys' Club, 'the Club' as it was fondly known, in Seville Place. The late, great Luke Kelly was also a member then, and he was always a great man to sing a song. With that mop of curly red hair and a voice that came from his boots, he delivered with a passion.

I won my first medal in the street leagues which were held in Sheriff Street playground and organised by our local

Gardai. In the fifties and sixties, many hours of harmless fun were had around the area of Seville Place, Sheriff Street, North Strand and East Wall.

Seán lived in Forth Avenue and was closely protected by his parents. However, he would always be allowed 'out' with me, for some reason. I think they thought I was sensible.

A crowd of lads was fishing in Spencer dock on the bridge at the end of Seville Place as Seán and I were flying by on bikes. One of the lads cast over his shoulder, and the hook caught Seán just over the eyebrow, causing the caster to run at break-neck speed. You might as well have tried to stop the B&I ferry as stop a bike in those days. Brakes? What are they?

We all cycled to the Mater (pronounced 'Matter'), hook in position over eye and rod on handlebars, and a hoard of 'hangers-on'. This was an event. I was thanked by his parents for 'looking after him'.

'Over the bridge' were the cattle pens, as exported cattle were 'hunted' loosely then down Seville Place and put into pens to await the cattle boat.

I called for Seán. We went 'over the bridge', Seán jumped into one of the empty pens right onto a six-inch nail sticking up from a pallet.

I gave him a crossbar to 'the Matter', complete with little plank and nail — I was thanked for 'looking after him'.

Another expedition, by bus, to the Phoenix Park. To save on the fare, we got off at the long-gone abattoir on the North Circular Road. We watched as the movement of live animals turned to dead ones and decided this needed investigation. Seán wound up in a vat of pigs' carcasses. Covered in blood and stinking to high heaven, we convinced the bus conductor (what's that?) to allow him a back seat on top. Seán looked like a corpse from a distance, which was the only way you could look at him. I was thanked for 'looking after him'.

Seán, wherever you are, leave your body to the College of Surgeons!

SINÉAD CUSACK

I was a very gloomy child. Deeply pessimistic and of an imaginative bent that can best be described as funereal. Hence any outing or treat arranged by my parents filled me with foreboding and the certain knowledge that somehow, the fun would pass me by.

One such treat I remember, planned with enormous care by my parents, was a day at the races for the whole family. What could be better? A lovely day at the Curragh, money to spend on the tote, picnics to be had in the grass and all the fun of the fair. My brother Paul fairly buzzed with excitement, my sister Sorcha glowed and sang with pleasure and I, well, I wept and wailed with all the anguish of a ten-year-old, sure that the luck would always be 'a-gin' me and no horse of mine could ever do anything except limp in last and probably have to be put down for its trouble.

I grizzled and groused and moaned and muttered all the way to the Curragh and successfully managed to dim everyone's enjoyment of the whole event. I was inconsolable, and by the time we got to the race course, so was everyone else.

Well, of course, I won. I won every race. My horses romped home. My winnings trebled, quadrupled and even accumulated. Nothing could stop me. My family watched in awe. I was a very impressive spectacle. They didn't like me very much, of course, but they were impressed. I should have learned a lesson that day — a lesson about optimism and hope. Did I learn it? Not at all.

I'm just the same as I was then. Sure that around the next corner, misery waits.

It's odd, really, because I've had a good life and I did win an awful lot of money at the races, but I still remain convinced that I'm doomed, that the Sword of Damocles will inevitably fall.

DEREK DAVIS

Remembered

My late father's family had a great seafaring tradition. His Uncle Robert, an old sea captain himself, used to set the exam papers for young officers taking their master's ticket, and my father's youngest brother was a head line-skipper when war broke out. That robust man survived the horrors of the Atlantic convoys despite the best efforts of German dive-bombers and U-boats but, to this day, he remains reluctant to talk about his experiences.

I reckon my father would have liked a career at sea himself, and his own family home was filled with memorabilia from the travels of his relatives. They had a summer house at Islandmagee near Whitehead in Co. Antrim, and it was a local joke that you had to have your master's ticket to get a house there.

My father was never happy far from the sea and though, as an adult, I fish rivers and lakes far from salt water, I share his passion for open seas, breaking surf and the cry of the sea birds — and why not? Because from our earliest days, any outing with my parents was to the seaside at Bangor or Donaghadee. Even on winter weekends, my sister and I would be loaded into the back of my father's Ford Prefect with the promise of an ice cream.

It was this habit that first brought me a close glimpse of tragedy and disaster. I'd heard my parents' talk, and my father's sombre tone told me that something dreadful had happened. The wireless, as well as the paper he brought home, were beyond my understanding, but there was a picture of a ship on the front page of the paper and bold headlines. The perfect tones of the news-reader spoke of the *Princess Victoria* and the dreadful loss of life — a storm in Belfast Lough . . . survivors . . . the local lifeboats . . . the worst in peace time since. . . .

Most of it made little sense to this toddler. I had no

experience of the war which had ended before I was born, except that certain vital items, especially sweets, were still rationed. Ice cream was not. The talk in the car between my parents was of the *Princess Victoria*. My father knew the vessel — it was the car ferry to England. It had carried troops during the war and its skipper was known to my father and his family as a fine seaman. It wasn't morbid curiosity. Our regular route to Donaghadee was along the coast and as we rounded a corner, there, in full view of the road, was a stretch of beach with ambulances lined up and men wading into the surf — the bodies were coming in on the tide. Quickly my father accelerated away. This was no sight for small children and my parents made no further comment in our hearing that day, though my father was quieter than usual.

I knew even then, from the effect on him, that something momentous had happened and my ears were tuned for any reference to the *Princess Victoria*. I gleaned other bits of information. The body of the Stormont Minister for Education, Sir Walter Smiley, had come up, almost at the back door of his own beautiful cut-stone house, near Donaghadee. Then there was the conversation between my father and his brother, the head line-skipper.

It can't have been too long after the disaster. It seemed that most of the survivors had been on lifeboats manned by the experienced ship's officers, men who had survived the convoys and winters in mid-Atlantic. The young men who had replaced the older crewmen at the end of the war did not have the experience, and many did not use the big sea anchors, submerged drogues that would pull the lifeboat around to face into a big sea. Their lifeboats were overwhelmed. Many died then, while others had been trapped below.

'And what happened to the old man?' my father asked, referring to the skipper.

'He was on the bridge as she went down. . . . He couldn't leave when there were still passengers and crew trapped below. . . . He saluted as she went under.'

That reply has chilled me for more than forty years — the rigid code of honour and the iron control of that valiant skipper as he chose death before the shame of abandoning those in his charge. I don't argue that his was a futile gesture, but it was brave beyond description. And when I read now of captains and crews who are first to the lifeboats when a cruise liner gets into trouble, I think of the old skippers, like the master of the *Princess Victoria*, with her loading doors smashed open and disaster inevitable, who couldn't place their own lives ahead of those whom they were charged to protect.

In later years, I tried to fathom that rigid code of honour. Perhaps the fate of Bruce Ismay, the owner of the great liner *Titanic*, gives some clue to the conduct of other sea-going folk in whose lifetimes that great disaster took place. It was alleged that Ismay had disguised himself as a woman to gain a place on one of the *Titanic's* lifeboats. His captain, the ship's designer and most of the senior officers perished. The press crucified Ismay and he fled to Connemara to hide his shame beside the famous Costello sea trout fishery. Ismay's disgrace was more than any honourable skipper could have faced. Maybe it crossed the mind of the brave man who saluted his vessel, and those still on board, as they all slid beneath the waves of a storm-tossed Irish Sea.

ÉAMON DE BUITLÉAR

The County brook, which divides Dublin from Wicklow, flowed past our bedroom window and the River Dargle, which was on the other side of the house, ran only a few yards beyond the kitchen.

Growing up in the Dargle valley meant that I always had

the sound of a waterfall in my ears, a lullaby without which I could hardly sleep. Most of the music came from the weir, a most magical place for wildlife.

This was where I grew up with my brothers and sisters, and it was on the banks of the river that we spent most of our playing time. My mother used to say that she should have grown a neck like a swan, from all the craning she did, watching to see if any of her brood had fallen into the water!

Above the weir, the river was flat and slow-moving. It seemed to hesitate before crossing this solid concrete barrier and then rushed down the moss-covered slope into two large fish pools below. Water-hens, wild duck and kingfishers nested along the flats above the tumbling cascade. A patient heron stood forever motionless at the edge. He was part of the landscape. He waited and waited at this spot, where some unsuspecting eel or trout with an urge to find new ground farther upstream would make the supreme effort of trying to swim up the fall. Quick as lightning, the grey statue would come to life as the victim was grabbed from the water by a rapier-like beak and swallowed head-first.

This part of the Dargle, where we lived, was a meeting place for a great variety of birds, insects, fish and mammals. The tumbling water suited many small aquatic animals, it had food for both fish and birds, and for the mammals it provided a crossing place. There were live wildlife programmes to be seen through our window every day. These sightings of animals were my first contact with what were to be many future friends.

In his spare time, my father fly-fished for trout and it was only natural that I, as a five-and-a-half year old, would want to do the same. I was duly supplied with a home-made rod on a particular day when the river was in flood, conditions which were more suitable for bait fishing than for the art of casting the artificial fly. A lowly worm was unceremoniously impaled for me on a small hook and I took up my position at the edge of the weir pool. This meant displacing the heron, who left hurriedly, squawking in protest as he flapped his way upstream. One could have felt sorry for him, as he seemed to hold a season ticket for this stand on the Dargle.

I imitated the heron by standing as he did, staring into the water, a small figure in bare feet with a long rod clutched in tiny hands trying to remain still. It must have been beginner's luck, because a sizeable brown trout, a pound in weight, grabbed my bait. Knowing nothing of what was happening down below me in the darkness of the murky pool, I attempted to lift my rod for another cast. It felt heavy and as I pulled and pulled again, suddenly the large trout came splashing and kicking and hurtling towards me. It was too much. With a gasp and a scream, I fled! In my wild panic, I forgot to drop my rod. Dragging the monster behind me, I tried to run backwards up the dry slope of the weir. Whatever disaster lay in store for this budding Isaac Walton and his catch was luckily averted by my father arriving just in time to save both boy and fish!

Anglers make good naturalists, as they spend many hours wandering along river banks or silently floating their boats on our many waterways. In those situations, they can observe much of the plant and animal life around them. Without the watchful eyes of these fishermen, many more Irish lakes and rivers would be lost to pollution.

The weir pool attracted quite a number of angling characters, including some local poachers. These Co. Wicklow fishermen were my first introduction to the many hidden secrets of the river.

There was Johnny, the motor mechanic, and little Ned from Kilkenny. Johnny had a smiling face and curly, dark hair. He always seemed black and oily, as if he had just left off repairing some engine before coming to fish. His long waders had lovely patches of the kind I had seen vulcanised on motor car tubes. Ned was thin, and as wiry as a whippet. He seemed to have an endless supply of check tweed caps and I never saw him without his essential piece of headgear, which was really so much a part of him. Ned used to

wonder at Johnny's talent as a tier of the most beautiful and
delicate of artificial flies. These were painstakingly made
from carefully chosen feathers and tinsels, silken threads
and tiny pieces of animal fur.

'How can a man with spades for hands, fashion such tiny
works of arts?' would be Ned's comment to another angler,
as Johnny, who had shown his flies to Ned, made his way
upstream to tempt some big trout with his latest insect
imitations.

Ned was a skilled tier himself and he specialised in
making colourful low-water salmon flies which were a joy
for any fisherman to have in his tackle box. He had the
biggest library of angling literature in the county and the
biggest collection of witty stories on the river.

Other piscatorial characters on the Dargle included the
poacher Harry and Hubert the gypsy. Hubert lived in a
horse-drawn caravan, close to the river. He was olive
skinned, and his accent was strange to me. I never saw him
on the river during the winter and it seems he spent that
part of the year trading in Wales. The family regarded
themselves as being of a much better class than the people
we knew in those days as 'tinkers'. I always enjoyed
watching Hubert fish his favourite bait, which was a wet fly
called the Orange Grouse. In order to attract the trout,
Hubert would jig the fly towards him, giving his line several
short, sharp pulls. The part of the activity which really
amused me, and which was always a part of the ritual, was
Hubert's way of calling 'troutee, troutee, troutee', in time to
the jigging line. Strangely enough, the technique seemed to
work as the bag on Hubert's shoulder was always full of
'troutees'.

It was from the poacher Harry that I learned the art of
fly-tying. He showed me how to make simple patterns of
small flies of the kind used generally in Co. Wicklow. They
all had names I could never forget — March Brown,
Greenwell's Glory, Bluebody Black Hackle, Red Spinner
and the Wicklow Killer. Harry taught me how to stalk trout
before casting a fly on the water. 'Walk very slowly and

quietly along the bank and keep your shadow off that part of the river,' he would say. 'Remember, trout can feel the vibrations as you walk along the bank.'

Otters have always lived in the Dargle. I often saw their signs and tracks in the mud and sand along the pools where they had been active the previous night. The poacher Harry often talked about their haunts and their angling abilities. They were really good fishermen, he told me. He also said that they were not really in competition with him, as otters preferred eels, whereas salmon and sea trout had far more appeal for him.

The school holidays were never long enough for us as there was always something to do on the river. A big wooden platform arrived on the weir one day. It had been carried down by the current, from somewhere farther afield. In the days ahead, it was to become a regular means of transport for us in the deeper waters above the weir. The unexplored wooded banks across the river now became the jungles of the Amazon as my brothers and I risked life and limb, dodging crocodiles and hippos as we poled our craft farther and farther upstream.

Whenever we were not aboard our craft, there were other ways in which we were to learn about life in the river. Building and dismantling dams was a regular pastime, and the lifting of rocks and stones revealed the hiding places of an endless variety of aquatic insects and small fishes. There were eels, baby trout, stone loach and lampreys. The harmless loach was known to the local boys as a 'stinger' because of its set of whiskers. They never referred to the lamprey as anything but a bloodsucker, because of this fish's habit of attaching itself to a stone by holding onto it with its mouth. The young mottled-brown herring gulls were called 'horse gulls', and siskins were known only as 'devines'. My favourite river birds were the kingfisher, because of its exquisite colouring, and the dipper, which amazed us all by regularly walking underwater in its hunt for caddis larvae.

The really exciting days on the Dargle were the flood times. It took two days of heavy rain to turn the Dargle from a small, clear and fairly easy-flowing river, into a mud-coloured, roaring torrent. As the water level rose rapidly, it had the effect of making the weir sink from view. The salmon pools then disappeared and the Dargle raced completely out of control, in a mad rush seawards.

For us, it was a good lesson in the power of water. Large trees growing farther upstream were torn from their stands along the river bank and came hurrying down like ancient craft, bobbing and dipping as if in salute to their small audience watching from the kitchen window. On one occasion, an unfortunate water-hen chose one of these floating trees as a perch. One could not tell when the unhappy passenger had gone aboard, but now it moved uncomfortably from branch to branch, wondering where to disembark. We all cheered as the multi-masted ship passed on downstream with the water-hen still on deck! I often wondered whether the bird eventually did get ashore or if it came to some unhappy end as the tree crashed its way past other obstacles farther downstream towards the town of Bray.

At its normal level, the Dargle was by no means a large river. In fact a Shannon-sider would almost certainly call it a brook. However, the Dargle River's small size was never an indication of its importance as a nursery for young salmon and sea trout. From April to May, the whole river seemed to teem with silvery smolt of about four to six inches in length. These were the fish which had changed their trout-like river outfits for sea suits of sparkling silver. They were baby sea trout and salmon answering to the call of the Atlantic and working their way downstream towards the estuary. These smolt would spend several years in the sea, even travelling as far north as Greenland in search of rich feeding. Eventually the urge to return would drive the salmon back in the direction of Ireland and instinct would then steer them towards their spawning beds in their native Dargle.

These were the magnificent fish that we would see from

our window, jumping, leaping and tumbling as they battled with their first obstacle since exchanging their saltwater habitat for a freshwater one. For these fresh-run salmon and sea trout, the weir was only a temporary barrier. They were as full of energy as the wild Atlantic which had fed them for the past few years. If the rush of water over the fall was too strong, they would try again and again, sometimes moving to another part of the weir to make another mighty leap into the swirling flood waters. It was a wonderful spectacle to watch.

The first migrants to arrive were the large sea trout of three and four pounds, which were the spring fish. They would usually swim into the first flood in June. In the following weeks would come the large runs of salmon weighing from six to twenty pounds and along with them would come, in their hundreds, the shoals of sea trout weighing anything from three-quarters of a pound to three pounds. These smaller sea trout, which were returning to the Dargle for the first time, were always known in the Bray area as 'clowns'. The name, according to my father, must have been in existence for a very long time, as 'clown' was really the Irish *caille abhainn*, river maiden, which is just what these fresh-run sea trout were!

That is part of what living and growing up in Co. Wicklow was for me. Little Ned used to say that whenever he was on a river, he was close to God, a sentiment which must have often had his angling audience wondering if God was a little deaf or if the sound of the weir drowned out the punch line in some of Ned's stories! The composer, Seán O Riada, who also fished with me on the Dargle, got musical inspiration from several rivers, including his own beloved Sullane in West Cork.

Whatever it is about our rivers and streams, I will be forever grateful that my parents decided to rear their family on the banks of the Dargle River.

From his book *Irish Rivers*

Proinsias De Rossa

Where I lived as a child, our playground on dry summer evenings was the street itself. In those days, Parnell Street, on Dublin's north side, was quiet after six o'clock but for bicycles and the odd 23 bus shuttling people to and from the Phoenix Park.

Occasionally, my parents would decide they had had enough of us, and head off to the pictures at the Royal. One of our older sisters would be put in charge, with strict instructions that we had to be in bed by eight.

She would have other ideas, of course. There was usually the lure of a dance somewhere that could not be missed. So the instructions would inevitably be passed down the line and just as inevitably ignored.

I remember one such evening particularly well. I must have been about nine years old. The evening was warm and the street was teeming with people of all ages, talking, walking, shouting and laughing. The youngsters playing 'pickie' and 'relievio', the youngfellas trick-acting with youngwans.

Someone had lifted the cover of the water hydrant at the corner of Ryder's Row opposite our house. They had put a piece of wood under it, jumped on the cover, and whoosh, we had our very own fountain.

Two dogs were doing what dogs do when in heat. While youngfellas were drenching them with basins of water from our new fountain, the adults watched, with amusement, the confusion of the poor animals which were now locked together in misery and pulling in opposite directions.

Suddenly, two women were shouting at each other and throwing their arms about trying to hit each other. It later transpired that one had impolitely requested that the other's mutt be restrained from interfering with her pet, which, unlike her, was unaccustomed to such daylight debauchery.

Everyone ran to watch this unexpected side-show. Some tried to get between the two women, got a belt and withdrew. Everyone forgot about the dogs.

As the crowd swelled, we couldn't see a thing, so we dashed inside and upstairs to our front room, where our windows gave us a balcony view of the action. We lifted a window and hung out, delighting in the frenzy below.

The two women swore and swung blows at each other, most of them missing their marks. But a hay-maker landed one of them on her backside. No sooner had she staggered back to her feet, than her large bloomers slid down to her ankles, the legs still held somewhere about her knees.

She looked around in panic, bent down, and pulling them to her waist, she dashed into the nearest hallway, banging the door behind her.

The crowd waited expectantly for a few minutes and then gave up. She did not re-emerge. The row was over. As the onlookers drifted away, the fire brigade arrived, bells ringing, and shut down our fountain.

Dusk was falling now and our minder still had not returned from the dance.

We scuttled off to bed. We didn't want to be around for the real row when our parents got home to find her missing — again. But there was no row that night. In fact, we would not see her again for a very long time. Our best pal had left for good. She had slipped away with her best pal to dance to her heart's content in pagan England.

JIMMY DEENIHAN

I suppose it is only natural that my childhood memories should centre around Gaelic football and those long summer days spent in the meadows saving hay, in the garden helping with the crops, or in the bog cutting and saving turf. They all bring back many happy memories.

It is difficult to relate to any one memory in particular. However, I do recall my first visit to Dublin with considerable sentiment. It was on the occasion of the Dublin/Kerry All-Ireland semi-final in 1959. My father, Mick, was a fanatical football enthusiast. His prime ambition for his only son was for him to play for Kerry, so he decided to introduce me to Croke Park at this early stage of my life. He also wanted to take me to see my Auntie Nell who lived in Dublin and who had not been back home in Kerry for some time. I remember vividly the feeling of elation that overcame me when he announced that I was to accompany him to Dublin. I bolted for the field at the back of the house with a ball and played an imaginary game of football between Kerry and Dublin until I was exhausted — Kerry, no doubt, having scored the last goal to win the game.

In those days we had a train service from Listowel. We got up at five o'clock on Sunday morning as the train was leaving at 6.30 am. I had never travelled on a train before so I was filled with curiosity and excitement.

When we arrived at the station the place was crowded. There were men there with peakie caps and hats, some wearing boots and many smoking pipes. I noticed a large number had their own sandwiches wrapped in newspaper in one pocket, together with a bottle of tea or milk in another pocket. The crowd was a mixture of young and old and were mostly males, many of whom were travelling to Dublin for the first time, like myself. No doubt we all shared the same sense of expectation and adventure for our first visit to the capital city. My father, who was a very popular man in GAA circles around North Kerry, met up immediately with a group from Moyvane and Ballydonogue with whom he had travelled previously to Dublin for big matches.

At that time, there were small carriages that would seat about eight people, so the company occupied one of these. I listened in awe and wonder at the stories that were told on the seven-hour trip to Dublin. Great matches were replayed, including the previous All-Ireland final in 1955 between Dublin and Kerry, when Kerry recorded a historical victory. Passing through Tralee and Killarney, we picked up people from West Kerry and South Kerry. A number of these were speaking Gaelic and were high in spirit. I recall vividly the dark, Spanish look of many of them which distinguished them from the North Kerry people.

Leaving Kerry for the first time had its own fascination. Millstreet, Mallow, Limerick Junction and the Curragh, places which I had seen on maps or heard about over the radio, suddenly became a reality. As we passed through each station, someone in our company was bound to associate a great footballer or hurler with that locality and a general conversation on his achievements would follow. All the diversions served to shorten the train trip and we were in Heuston Station before we knew where we were. I recall the atmosphere and the air of excitement in the train when the announcement — 'Heuston next stop' — came out over the public address system. A state of frenzy gripped the train and exclamations like 'Come on, Kerry!' and 'Up the Kingdom!' could be heard coming from every carriage. They could not wait to get to Croke Park when they hit the platform.

My father's two nephews, Frank and Tommy Geoghegan, collected us at the station. Before they took us to see Auntie Nell, they gave us a tour of Dublin. On our way from the station, the first place we passed was Guinness's brewery. I remember my father remarked, 'That is where we get all our medicine in Kerry from.' It was only years afterwards that I fully appreciated his comment.

Having completed the tour of all the sights to be seen in Dublin at that time, including the Dáil where Frank worked, we arrived in my auntie's house for dinner. There was a tremendous reception and all the Geoghegan family was there to greet us. My father was a big hero in the Geoghegan family household, as all the nephews spent their summer holidays in Kerry with him and had great memories of working on the farm at home, fishing in the River Feale or swimming in Ballybunion.

When lunch was over and gifts exchanged, we headed to Croke Park. On the way to the game we listened to the build-up by Michael O'Hehir, a great man to create an atmosphere for the big occasion. When we reached Jones's Road, the place was a mass of flag-waving supporters from Dublin and Kerry. The stage was set for an epic encounter.

And so it was — one of the greatest matches ever played, with Kerry winning by just two points in front of a record crowd for a semi-final. Commenting on the match, the distinguished reporter, John D. Hickey of the *Irish Independent* said: 'Although the passage of time hallows memories, causes one to rate good matches great and great matches epics, I have no doubt that yesterday's majestic All-Ireland senior semi-final at Croke Park was the best, the most enthralling and the most incident-packed football encounter that I have ever seen.'

I may have played in great games since, but I must say that I never felt the same euphoria and excitement as a spectator as I felt during this game. It was also the greatest game Micko Connell ever played for Kerry — his fielding and kicking were just majestic.

Leaving behind my cousins and the excitement of Croke Park may have been somewhat of an anti-climax. The train journey home was long and tedious, despite the jubilant Kerry supporters. Eventually we arrived home at about two o'clock in the morning.

It was a great experience and memory. The last thing my father said to me before we went to bed was, 'I hope that I will be going to Croke Park to see you playing some day.'

Now, in retrospect, I fully realise how fortunate I was to have made that unforgettable excursion with my father. His spirit must have been with me when I played for the Kingdom in all those All-Ireland campaigns.

RONNIE DELANY

Growing up in Sandymount, Dublin 4, was a lifetime experience. So many things happened then and have remained in my memory down the years.

We moved from Arklow in 1939 to Melrose, St John's Road. My first school was St Mary's, Haddington Road, where I made my First Communion, as they used to say. Two things flash before my mind's eye. First, there was Marie O'Reilly from up the road and myself heading off on that very special day, dressed like bride and groom to receive the sacrament. Afterwards, a bag of sweets which I shared with all and sundry, and to my horror, even the adults took one. It was so painful having to grow up, but for the first time in my life I felt I was a little man. Such chivalry and generosity taught to us by the gentle Sisters of Mercy were to remain part of my persona, I believe.

My more liberal education was taken care of by spending endless hours in the local cinema, popularly known as the 'Shack'. Entrance was gained, I recall, for a few pence or a couple of returnable jam jars. There was an endless run of cowboy films and local reputations were built by being fast on the draw. It was the way you wore your Colt .45 that mattered, more especially as the explosive caps were in short supply. Our celluloid heroes were matched only by the legendary character, Bang-Bang, who rode into town on the platform of the No. 7 tram, shooting anything that moved. You survived on your ability to take cover whenever he was on the rampage. And happily, he was never caught and was last seen riding off into the sunset.

The popular comic books of the day were readily exchangeable, so reading material was in plentiful supply. Johnny Forty Coats, an eccentric old man so attired, and an avid reader, was always ready to do a swap if you had the tenacity to barter with him. Word spread rapidly when he was in the Sandymount area and the brave-hearted sought him out to do a trade. Johnny only supplied the latest comics with, I am certain, a twinkle in his eye. I wonder whatever happened to him and Bang-Bang. Who were they and why were they so odd and yet so much part of my earliest days and now my fondest memories?

Celluloid and print! Sound came next in the magical form of the radio, static and all. Such imagination was required to picture Madison Square Garden and the heavyweight championship of the world. The excitement of getting up in the middle of the night and the opportunity, unknowingly, to bond with Daddy for life. A hastily-lit fire, perhaps a cup of tea, and then the fight. Enthralled by the commentary and inter-round summaries, only to be aghast when the Fighting Irishman, Billy Conn, is knocked cold by the Brown Bomber, Joe Louis. Or to hear that 'the British boy, Bruce Woodcock, is boxing magnificently, with beautiful straight lefts', but suddenly to learn that he is flat on his back. Such drama and excitement unmatched by even today's live satellite transmissions.

Remarkably, perhaps, I have no unhappy memories of my childhood. But on reflection, it is no wonder, for we had so much to do and see. Or perhaps I should have said 'hear'.

The world is such a beautiful place for children, so full of fantasy and dreams, today and every day.

MICK DOYLE

A Memory from a Kerry Childhood

I find that most memories from my childhood in Kerry are highly evocative, prompting quite incredible nostalgia, a longing to relive times past, and sadness for those family and friends who have passed on. I suppose age has something to do with it.

Although a Kerryman by birth and inclination, if not by profession, I have been living in Kildare for most of my life. I do intend, however, to go back to live in South Kerry quite soon, where I hope I will sit in the evenings looking out over the Kenmare River in the environs of Parknasilla and long for former times in Kildare! I will then have memories from two great places.

It is quite funny how certain prompters begin the flow through the memory pathways — almost like those futuristic computer super highways. Some memories can be fleeting, relived in milliseconds, while others are savoured by the brain's flavour-meter and lived through as if they had happened yesterday.

Every time I smell newly-mown hay, for example, I am transported back to Currow village, to my Uncle Bill Dennehy's farm and the endless summers 'saving' hay. (With the unpredictability of the weather in this country, one doesn't 'make' hay, one 'saves' it.) Uncle Bill would cut the hay, going around the headland twice to get a good run at the whole meadow. Two horses, one black and one roan, pulled the mowing machine with its nostalgic clackety-clack mowing-bar action.

As the meadow in each field was being mowed, us cousins — Tom, Hugh, Liam and myself — went around looking for corncrake nests, trying to save them from the mower blades. We failed now and then but often discovered wild honey hives deep in the ground which we dug up, bees permitting.

When the hay was cut, it was aerated by tossing and turning with the sward-turner — referred to as 'the cock pheasant'. This ingenious machine, like a series of lawn rakes on wheels, did a great job of drying wet hay.

Us youngsters' main job was to make grass cocks of the drying hay by gathering it up with two-prong pikes or forks. If the weather was not at its best, these had to be turned every day to get the best drying.

When Uncle Bill decided that it was dry enough, we then began the serious business of making the big wynds that used to be such a feature of the Irish countryside before mass silage-making.

First, the grass cocks were gathered together into rows throughout the meadow by means of a horse-drawn, steel hay-rake, a simple but extraordinarily effective piece of machinery. This helped to dry the hay further and allow for easier wynd-making.

The other horse was tackled to a wooden rake called a 'skeeter' which brought the hay to exactly the correct spot for each wynd.

I loved using the steel rake, clearing up the last vestiges of hay from each meadow.

Making the wynds called for traditional expertise; the preparation of the correct base with a slope towards the centre was crucial.

A couple of us youngsters were required to stand on the rising 'pile', compressing it for stability and eventual shape as it was brought expertly to a rounded peak. It was then raked with wooden rakes to ensure a smooth outer layer of interwoven hay to make it rainproof.

Tying the wynd down against the wind was the final act of acute interest and importance. It was great to finish each whole meadow and leave the greenish-yellow dried hay to 'mature' in its wynds over the summer.

Billy-cans of tea, and ham, egg and tomato sandwiches never smelled or tasted so good as those during hay-making. A swim in the Flesk River during a break in the sweaty proceedings was better than in any Riviera swimming pool. The race back to the farmyard to get the cows in for evening milking was more fun than any dodgem cars.

I was lucky even when I didn't realise it back then. My older children saw hay-baling and silage-making when they were growing up, but they missed a part of Irish life that is sadly almost gone forever. I wouldn't have missed it for anything. Thankfully, the fields in South Kerry are still small enough in places to deter the silage-makers and on a June morning, should you cycle from Kenmare to Sneem or get out of your car for a minute, you will smell the heady aroma which I guarantee you will never forget.

Lawn-mowing comes a poor second!

RODDY DOYLE

I am lying on a mattress. My brother is asleep beside me. It isn't our usual room or my usual bed. Just a mattress on the floor. There is a window above me. A perfect block of sunlight stands in front of me. The dust dances through it. I am very happy. The door opens; it creaks. It is right behind me. I look back and see my mother's aunt, Bessie. She smiles at me. I hear my father laughing downstairs.

Kilmuckridge, Co. Wexford: summer — probably 1963

JOE DUFFY

Clattering out of the Gala Cinema, jockeying my imagination bareback as Geronimo Duffy wreaked havoc up the Ballyfermot Road — these are my earliest childhood memories.

Searching through the kaleidoscope of my memory, I can find myself standing in Parliament Street in Dublin in June 1963, waving a plastic tricolour, as a handsomely sun-tanned John F. Kennedy cavalcaded through the thronged streets. Even then, at seven-and-a-half years of age, I could feel that the presidential home-coming was a watershed in the life of the Irish state. Not long afterwards, I can recall my father refusing to bring us to the annual Easter military parade because he had heard from a fella in the know that the IRA would attack on the fiftieth anniversary of 1916.

Watching the parade on television and above all the exotic military trucks, we waited for the expected onslaught, jeering the foolishness of the crowds — what stupid, uninformed parents they must have!

Alas — but thankfully — the IRA failed to materialise on Clery's roof and we missed a brilliant parade.

St Patrick's Day was another highlight, mainly because my uncle drove a brand new Massey Ferguson tractor in the parade — forget your horse-drawn coach, your exotic displays; the highlight was Uncle Jerry on his brand-new tractor.

The cold ice cream headache we got from Forte's Café in O'Connell Street was as important a part of the parade as the marching bands, as was standing outside O'Meara's public house on Bachelor's Walk, clutching a small bottle of Club Orange, sipping from a straw, fingering a bag of King Crisps, waiting for my father to emerge from the smoky cave and bring us home.

Outside O'Meara's public house and saloon bar, we were in the care of the fruit seller. Our father accompanied us on the bus to Ballyfermot, but left us in the care of the conductor as he departed for his regular home, Downey's, for the final leg of the journey.

Childhood memories are always evoked by smells — lavender polish on a scrubbed doorstep; the smell of a newly-painted room meant Christmas was coming; the pungent aroma of Windolene heralded the arrival of the summer holidays.

Adventuring around the fields behind our house in Ballyfermot — the Backers, now a prison — will always be the freedom motif of childhood summers. The sad memories reside in my complete inability to play sports; standing in line to be picked for a football game on the local green was a nightmare. Eventually, after all the boys and girls were picked, I would be left standing with the local dog — Ringo. Skulking off, I remember the lift in my little heart as I was called back — 'Joe, Joe, come back! Ringo's picked!'

Joe Duffy, aged thirty-nine-and-a-half

BISHOP JOSEPH DUFFY

Lost and Found

My cousin Paddy died last year. It fell to me to celebrate the funeral Mass and to recall, for his family and friends, memories of our childhood together many years ago.

One story that I did not tell, because it was not suitable for adults, was about the day we got lost in Croke Park. Paddy was twelve and I was ten and our daddies had brought us to Dublin on the train to see the Railway Cup finals which used to be held every year on St Patrick's Day. During the war years, the railway was our normal means of travel and a visit to Dublin usually meant the adventure of spending a night or two in a small hotel near what was Amiens Street station. A feature of the city at that time were the air-raid shelters in the middle of the streets, big concrete bunkers that were removed as soon as the war was over.

How we got lost was very simple. There was a separate entrance to the park for schoolboys, which meant that we joined a crowd of youngsters like ourselves and almost immediately became invisible to anyone looking out for us. We knew that our new companions were Dubs because they had Dublin accents and we were fascinated by that. But then, suddenly, we realised that we were lost and we did not know what to do. We began to walk and then to run. The first match began, but the excitement of the play and of the spectators passed us by. We then got frightened and became convinced that we would never see our parents again. We got tired running and sat down on the cold steps. The feeling was that the world had stopped and that the crowds of people around us were miles and miles away. We were unable to say a word to each other.

After what seemed an age, a man came towards us and asked us if we were two boys who were lost. Our fathers had been frantic looking for us and, like us, had got no pleasure from the match. They had notified the stewards who, in the absence of a public address system, set out to find us.

Every time I hear a message over the system at a football match for children who have got detached from their elders, I think of two small boys from the country in Croke Park on St Patrick's Day all those years ago.

In a more prayerful moment, I think of the boy in the gospel who got lost in a strange country and eventually, after much unhappiness, found his way home. There are few tears of joy to compare.

EILEEN DUNNE

One of my earliest memories is of journeys to and from Clonmellon in Co. Meath where my maternal grandmother lived. To get there from our home in Dublin, we drove to Navan, then Kells and on to Clonmellon. Between Navan and Kells, there's a stretch of road where the trees from both sides meet to form an archway for the passing cars. Late at night, particularly around Christmas-time, if it was frosty, this archway looked white in the glare of the headlights, and with the stars twinkling overhead it was quite magical!

There are three of us; I'm the eldest. And as we drove along, my father would regale us with stories about the 'gingerbread men' who lived at the bottom of our garden. Being the good journalist he is, these gingerbread men were as real as the relatives we had just left behind, and I would imagine them on frosty nights under the stars, and feel sorry for them.

When the latest episode in the lives of this family ended, my father would turn to my mother and say, 'Are they asleep yet, Lilly?' I would pipe-up, 'No,' and he would be forced to start all over again!

Many things have changed since. For a start, I now work shift-hours and would sleep anywhere, any time! My grandmother has died and the house in Clonmellon has been sold, so I rarely travel that road nowadays. But when I do, it's of gingerbread men and white nights that I'm thinking!

DESMOND EGAN

First day at school
(*What is imagination but memory?* James Joyce)

Childhood: the time when we are fully alive. Can we ever recover that? Or ever stop trying to?

So many sharp memories. The smell of comics in Walsh's shop on Thursdays. Old Mr Fitz (younger than I am now) reciting 'She is far from the Land' passionately to our class, changing us a little for keeps. The family rosary, with one or other of us sniggering. My father's Austin A40 being polished down the back lane. Our street thronged with horses for the January fair when we had to get a free day. Stamps. Frankie Hayden's meccano set made into a projector and Frankie humming the signature tune for the ads. Flowers and scents all over the kitchen for the Procession. My Auntie Maggie and my mother having a cushion fight over little me! The raw glare in the sky that night the cotton factory burned down. Those half-epilepsies when the utter strangeness of everyone else made me a sudden outsider and the world swing away. A girl singing 'One Day when We were Young' walking down an empty street that was summer and all the summers in Athlone.

The first day at school, though: that was special. Everything about it, now. The feel of new clothes. My father wetting tea, humouring us, my mother and me. Special sandwiches cut special for me, wrapped fresh with love. My father holding two-year-old Tomás, waving from the shop door. The twelve miles to Tang, new as the schoolbag — and my mother turning into a teacher in front of my eyes! Some hint of loneliness caught in a bend of the road. The schoolhouse, so self-contained, its upper storey of windows and secrets.

Then country faces and girls and ancient smells. The threat of sums (an otherness I was resisting) on a swing blackboard. Another teacher's unconvincing smile. The wooden breath of the room. A bench with iron in it. Inkwells that had sliding brass covers — why? A new ritual, its high windows already pushing back the world of childhood. A seat polished by the reality adults knew about. Chalk dust. A knot in the cold floor and in me.

Before the sos into my total shyness and its anxiety to please (did I ever recover?)

Later the lunch that made me a grown-up, with the tea steaming from my mother's flask: O that unhot, acidy taste which can still lift me back, as a song can, into a lost world. A state of protectiveness and discovery, of delight and fear, of questions which had answers; somewhere you could be utterly astonished: a bridge with a drowned kitten; the tree in the school yard, swarming with beetles; the whistle of corduroy.

A first day which is hardly decipherable, like the ghost of

chalk-writing, dusted over carelessly by time — and I feel at this moment a rush of compassion for that solemn, lanky, half-stranger with the far-too-dreamy face that was just asking for it, and the hopes that could never be realised.

BRIAN FARRELL

Earliest Memories of Dublin

For a small boy reared in the Irish ghettos of Manchester, the promise of a visit to Dublin was full of magical anticipation. My mother's people came from the West; born in Sligo, reared in Mayo, until the whole family emigrated. Dad's folk had moved from Wicklow before he was born in Glasgow. So really we were country people by background, plonked down in the middle of a heavily industrialised and grossly polluted English industrial city.

We kept up country ways. On both sides, an extended family meant that much of the social week — such as it was — turned into a round of visits by tram to grandparents, aunts and uncles. Friends visited on what I later came to recognise as the *cuairt*. There would be cups of tea and chat and, if the grown-ups were in good form, an impromptu concert of ballads and come-all-ye. And, as the night wore on, there would be stories of 'home' — and that always meant Ireland.

At the time, I scarcely valued the folk memories so casually tossed about. It was talk of 'the city' (and that always meant Dublin) that caught my attention and fired my imagination. I quickly learned that the Liffey ran right through the streets and had images of a kind of Venice where you might step off the pavement and into the water. And I knew there was a huge park with a statue. And it was all beside the sea.

My aunt, who would later rear me, brought me over to Dublin in 1937. It was the greatest journey in the world for an eight-year-old. The train steaming up, as I clutched the precious half-crowns pressed into my hands on farewell. The bustle of the great port of Liverpool and the enormous bulk of the spanking-new *SS Munster* towering over the quay-side.

Inside it was like a liner. Lovely panelled corridors, white-coated stewards and the neatly organised intimacy of the cabin, through the port-holes the twinkling lights of the shore quickly receding. I munched on my Smith's crisps (they still put the salt in a separate screw of blue paper inside the bag), delighted to be going home to Ireland and to the excitement of the city.

I didn't want to sleep, in case I should miss some of the fun. But somehow or other, even on board the ship, the sandman made the rounds. Suddenly I was shaken awake. The sun was beaming a slant of brilliant light through the port-hole. Jump into clothes and rush on deck for a first glimpse of Ireland.

Howth, majestic and beautiful as ever, hiding the bay for a minute. Then that sweep around Baily and the south of the Liffey beckoned us into the heart of the city. Sailors are about their mysterious business with ropes. The ship glides into the tranquil waters along the quays, across from the long finger of the gasometer pointing into the sky. There are strange, different smells here. People look different. And, as we step into the cobbled street, the horse-drawn cabs promise that everything will be different.

Along the quays and its horse-drawn traffic everywhere. Trams and buses are green, with colourful advertisements along their sides, almost garish after the solid, stolid, unadorned red of the Manchester public transport livery. The river is a disappointment. It doesn't lap up against the pavement after all but is neatly contained behind strong stone walls, just like the Manchester Ship Canals. But there are swans and the busy Guinness lighters, steaming along with their precious cargo.

My aunt had a little dairy, the Market Dairy, in Little Mart Street, just beside the fruit and vegetable market. That was a world I'd soon come to explore and own as my own. The old ladies (they were probably in their thirties) selling second-hand clothes in the Daisy market and earning strange nicknames — 'Maggie All-Wool's' name explained itself. The banks of flowers and baskets of fruit. And, all about, a meeting of city and country, accents, horses, men and women like some massive film set of a mighty epic.

The place teemed with life. It spilled over from the families, crowded into single rooms in the tenement houses with their open hall-doors and red-raddled stairways. It shouted with the calls of the dealers as they pushed their loaded carts to Moore Street. It knocked, before seven o'clock in the morning, on the still-closed doors of the 'market houses', pubs that were licensed to open early to meet the needs of the market workers but which were oases drawing early-morning drinkers from all over the city.

Within days, the promised visit to the park. That was another bit of disappointment at first. I rode the carrier on the back of my uncle's bike. Into the Conyngham Road gate, passed the Wellington obelisk and hop off to admire the Gough statue. It took me a bit of time to work out why it wasn't a massive cat. (I had heard so much talk about the Felix Park that I assumed it was dedicated to the cartoon character, Felix the Cat.) But I soon got over that and marvelled as we trundled on and on, with great fields on either side and across the Fifteen Acres to creep stealthily up on the unsuspecting deer. And then back to the Dog Pond and our handsome collie, with its strangely fore-shortened tail, called Trust, ready to spend all day plunging in to fetch a stick cast upon the waters.

It was all so simple. Such a long time ago. To discover that the open fields as well as the crowded streets were part and parcel of what was to become my Dublin, and my home.

FRANK FEELY

I was eight years of age when I succumbed to the lure of the spotlights. The venue was no Carnegie Hall, but the hall of the Christian Brothers' School about two miles from my home.

Each Sunday afternoon for a couple of pence, one could enjoy a cine-variety show here. The cinematic end of it consisted of black-and-white cartoons and short films, generally comedies. Occasionally, as a very special treat, one might see a full-length 'B' film. The mainstay of the variety programme was a talent competition, the participants being children.

It was here, on one such afternoon, that I found myself lined up on the stage, persuaded, though not altogether unwilling, by my buddies to unleash my talents on the unfortunate audience. I was part of what seemed like a conveyor belt of children moving slowly to the right until one reached the microphone to do his or her piece and move on. I knew one song which I still remember: 'The day is ended, little drummer boy; lights out have sounded long ago . . .' etc.

To my consternation, I heard the girl immediately in front of me, when her turn came, belt out this self-same song. I remonstrated with the MC, muttering about people stealing other persons' songs, and was allowed to sing the same song again.

When the results were declared, I was runner-up and received, as a prize, the princely sum of two shillings and sixpence. I remember harbouring some resentment against the winner on two scores. He was about fourteen years of age, which seemed like another generation to an eight-year-old, and he sang what seemed to me a rather up-market song: 'Sing sing, Vienna mine; round me a garland of roses twine . . .' etc.

Nevertheless, I had visions of a lucrative career, taking

part each Sunday in this variety contest.

This dream, however, was shattered the following Sunday when, while attempting to climb on the stage, I was greeted by shouts of 'He was up last week!' and disbarred on the basis of being a previous winner. I had made the fatal mistake of again wearing my black-and-white herringbone pattern overcoat with the large leather buttons which could be clearly seen from a distance of half a mile, even in dense fog, thereby affording instant recognition.

Thus ended my short-lived career on the stage.

GARRET FITZGERALD

Hens I have known — and other animals

S ome of my earliest memories are about hens. Several times between the ages of two and four, I stayed either with friends of my parents in Bray or at a hotel in Greystones — while my parents were moving house to Bray and later when they were away on holidays on the Continent.

My earliest memory of all is, I think, of hens in the back garden of Mrs Somers' house in Bray. Mrs Somers was the station-master's widow in whose house my father had stayed for a while in December 1914, after being expelled from Kerry by the Royal Irish Constabulary (RIC).

(His expulsion, incidentally, had been because of hens. My mother, fearing an egg shortage during the Great War, decided to keep hens, and the RIC across the bay in Ventry had mistaken the light of my mother's lantern, as she fed her hens late at night, for an attempt by my father, organiser of the Volunteers in West Kerry, to signal to German submarines. I owe the fact that I am a Dubliner rather than a Kerryman to this error.)

In 1914, Mrs Somers' house (in which a centenarian

daughter of hers still lives) was the 'safest' house in Bray for a rebel. As she and her parents had been evicted from Coolgreany in Co. Wexford in 1887, she was correspondingly hostile to the British regime and sympathetic to the Irish Volunteers. Her back garden abutted on the railway line which, for a two-year-old, added to the excitement of the hens, which I was allowed to feed.

A year or two later I stayed at the Clydagh Hotel in Greystones, looked after by my nurse while my parents were away. The hotel had several wooden hen-houses and I was allowed to collect the eggs from them each day — an immense privilege. This hotel was also near the railway line and I recall being greatly impressed one day when a train stopped opposite the hotel to pick up a man waiting on the track. I remember wondering just how important one would have to be for a train to stop especially in this way.

Later, at our house outside Bray, my mother decided to raise twenty-six chicks and six ducklings for the table. I could recall the macabre business of seeing a chicken killed and the exciting business of plucking it. But before we got much value out of these fowl, I woke up one morning and, looking out of the nursery window towards the paddock where the fowl-run was situated, I saw all the chickens and ducklings lying dead — killed by a fox.

When the Second World War broke out, my mother decided once again to ensure against an egg shortage by buying a dozen hens. The space available in the garden in Temple Road, Rathmines, was limited so she ensured their good health by hanging cabbages over their heads which they had to jump up and down to peck at. I had to mix the feed for the hens and give it to them each day — a task which I addressed with much less enthusiasm as a teenager than I had done as a very small child, especially as I also had to water sixty-three chrysanthemums near the hen-run as well as the countless plants in the greenhouse.

I also had to feed my guinea pig — until one day our cat got at it in its hutch on the lawn and killed it. (The guinea pig's name was Mrs Ezra Pound; as we were walking past the GPO one day, my father suggested the name Ezra Pound because the poet had been a friend of his in London before he and my mother came to live in Kerry in 1913, but he hadn't realised that the guinea pig was female.)

We had been told that the guinea pig would be useful because it would eat the dandelions in the lawn. The trouble was that it was a fast eater, so my father and I had to go out regularly along the Rathmines' roads looking for dandelions in the crevices of walls and pavements to bring back to Mrs Ezra Pound. During one such foraging operation, we found a hedgehog and brought it home, where it remained for some time, keeping the guinea pig company. When they were joined by a neighbouring cat, which, despite the fact that we already had a cat of our own, chose to have kittens in our coal-shed, and by a holidaying brother's dog, we briefly had quite a menagerie — about which my mother, who basically did not like animals, was notably unenthusiastic!

EOGHAN FITZSIMONS

The Seventh Green

As a ten-year-old, my golf clubs — six in all — were hickory shafted, with the driver being made entirely of wood. The latter had been crafted and varnished by the then Sutton professional. I was there when he handed it — along with the other clubs — to my father in his workshop, which was small and dark and very humble indeed by modern standards.

Mind you, at the time the clubhouse in Sutton was also fairly humble. Corrugated iron, painted red but reduced to terracotta by the elements, coated the exterior. Permeating the interior was a curious, though not unpleasant, smell of what seemed like a mixture of polish, beer, leather and cut grass. The main room was fairly dark but Joe Carr's enormous trophies shone there with a pride which we were all happy to share. There was also a bright sitting room overlooking the ninth green, cheerfully furnished with chintz-covered armchairs. Photos and prints decorated the walls and were endlessly examined. Team pictures, in two of which my mother featured, were prominent.

The seventh green was my favourite. It always seemed so sheltered. On a warm summer's morning, save for the occasional strident gull, it was the quietest place on earth. To a ten-year-old golfer, golf was, of course, more important than silence and peace. Indeed at the time, it ranked as the most important activity of all.

I took great pride in my clubs. They were kept clean and varnished when not in use. My favourite was the mashie niblick, the equivalent of the modern seven iron. I used it for chipping, long and short. The seventh green was a regular venue for practice. Chipping was practised into the wind, against the wind, uphill, downhill, wet and dry, from bank, bunker and rough. When the ball could not be placed within two feet of the hole, there was something very wrong indeed.

After golf in those days, it was off to the golf books. My uncle had a collection of books on his heroes. Thus the golfing lives of Henry Cotton, Gene Sarazen, Harry Vardon and others, with the magic of the far-off places that they conjured up, served to inspire practice for the next day.

The intensity of my youthful interest in golf reached a peak during my eleventh year and then waned, with tennis gradually taking over. Tennis — on grass — was a wonderful substitute. I cannot say, however, that it ever received the same intense dedication as did that mashie niblick at the seventh green in Sutton.

ROGER GARLAND

Although born in India, I have to confess to being a real Dub — fifth generation at least. My childhood, apart from the first six months, which I naturally don't remember, was spent in Dublin, with occasional forays to other parts of Ireland. These forays were quite rare because, in common with others in my age group, it was not easy to get about during the war, or should I say 'the Emergency', as it was rather quaintly described in official circles.

Dublin during the war was a very different place from what it is today. In many ways it was much better than today. No problems with emissions from car exhausts as there were no private cars in those days, and even before the cars went off the road about 1941, most people used the train, the tram, the bike or foot power to get to work. Mind you, Dublin was a lot smaller then and few people, other than those in Dun Laoghaire, or Kingstown as it was still called by some of the old-timers, lived quite close to the city centre.

As far as I was concerned, the bike was king. Cycling to school. On Sundays, cycling with my father with fishing rods tied to the cross-bar or off to Co. Wicklow for holidays. Into the guard's van with the bike and then off at Rathdrum and, having loaded up the panniers, we had a pleasant enough cycle to Glendalough, Laragh or Glenmalure. The hills were sheer hell though — none of your 25-gear jobs then!

Cycling, however, wasn't always a bed of roses. The volume of traffic was light but tram-lines were the bugbear. Despite strictures from my mother, 'Mind the tram-lines,' somehow I was always getting my wheels jammed, followed by a crashing 'over the handle-bars' fall. No safety helmets in those days!

Probably the greatest thrill was travelling by train or

even just going to the station to see the trains, or rather the engines. Steam engines were a tremendous fascination for me. They had real character, not like the anonymous diesel engines of today. When they suddenly 'let off steam', they made a woeful racket and used to frighten the living daylights out of me. Even though I knew the big hiss was imminent, I was always unprepared and with loud sobs, I would bury my head in my father's coat. A classic example of a love-hate relationship!

As well as cycling, we also used the train a lot. In fine weather, a trip to the beach at Killiney was always made by train. The tunnel under Killiney Head really made the trip. But the daddy of them all was the outing to Greystones. Now there's tunnels for you — must be half a dozen under Bray Head. Another favourite was the trip on the Howth Head tram. As far as I remember, the Howth tram survived well into the fifties and its closing down was an act of environmental vandalism of the first order.

Now, I could go on about seeing my first banana just after the war, but I'll leave that for another day!

CHRIS GLENNON

Passions

Aunt Mary had two passions — religion and racing. She attended 8.30 Mass every morning and, on her return home, immediately took up the paper to study the racing entries and form. It seemed as if praying and betting went together; at least that's the way it appeared to the small boys of the household. Our aunt, who lived with us, prayed every day at Mass and had a bet every day in the bookies. I never remember her going to a race meeting, not even to Naas, less than a mile from where we lived.

The nearest she'd get to participation in a race meeting would be to watch the traffic to and from Punchestown, at that time a once-a-year meeting in late April.

Strange as it seems some fifty years on, hundreds of people would stand at vantage points in Naas to watch the few motor cars or buses and the huge numbers of horse carriages, traps, cyclists and walkers head off for the national festival of hunt racing.

One year, just after the end of the 1939–45 war, there was a genuine stagecoach, pulled by four horses and with a man sitting on top blowing a bugle to signal its passage through the town.

We walked to Punchestown, up the Craddockstown Road, known locally as the Poor House Road because, in the previous century, the homeless, the abandoned and the ill were taken in there and given a roof over their heads. We watched the races at Punchestown, walking out to the Double Bank or the Stone Wall where there often was real action. We never thought of it as callous that we were unmoved by horses being so severely injured that they had to be put down. To us, it meant that in the following day or two, we'd 'help' Theo Higgins, John Breen or some of the men from the Kildare Hunt Club to bring the carcasses to the kennels to feed the hounds or to the knackers' yard.

Rarely we would have a bet on a horse, usually on the tote where the minimum wager was two shillings. A bet depended on a tip from my dad, a noted student of the turf, or Uncle Mick, a shoemaker by trade, a professional gambler by instinct. The bets were peripheral to the enjoyment of the two days off school, the racing and the fun and games on the way out and home. Anyway, money seemed too precious to put on a horse that could so easily fall. There were sweets to be bought, goes to be had on the swinging boats, the chair-o-plane and such. And if Aunt Mary's bets in the bookies came up, there was the certainty that we would be beneficiaries. She always gave us money from her winnings.

If we ourselves bet on anything at that time, it usually was when we raced polish boxes on the river alongside the Ballymore Road, coincidentally another route to Punchestown. The empty boxes were gathered from our homes, and anyone who wanted to enter put up a ha'penny or a penny. The starter threw all the boxes in together and whichever got down to the corner opposite Corcorans' house was the winner. There was a more difficult course on a stream that ran into Well Lane and into the canal; it went underground twice and often boxes, ha'pennies and pennies disappeared, never to be seen again. It was great when you won a race, since it put you in funds, as we called it, for about a week; eight or nine pence went a long way then.

I had only four pence when I reached what seemed then to be a critical point in my footballing career. I was included in the group of primary schoolboys practising for the under-14 team. But I had no proper football boots. I told Dad I needed boots and shorts if I was to have a chance of making the team. He gave me a penny to add to the four I had — and the names of three horses to be ridden in England that day by the great Gordon Richards.

I invested the shilling in a treble and, passing the church, the association of Aunt Mary's praying and betting came to mind. I went in and said a prayer for Gordon Richard's treble.

I got thirty-seven shillings, nearly £2, when he romped home. And that bought not alone the boots and shorts but the proper football socks as well.

We went on to win the under-14 Kildare county championship.

TONY GREGORY

Like generations of children before me in Dublin's north inner city, I was educated by the Christian Brothers.

I lived in Ballybough, overlooking the railway line and the Royal Canal, just ten minutes' walk to St Canice's CBS. St Canice's was the poor relation of the adjoining O'Connell's primary school which attracted the better-off children from as far away as Howth.

'Caniers' had a green blazer and cap as school uniform, which almost no one wore, simply because our parents could not afford such luxuries and it was not expected of us by the Brothers. By way of contrast, all the boys in O'Connell's arrived at school each morning in their bright red blazers and caps, neatly trimmed with gold braid.

When snow was on the ground, we took great delight in pelting the 'posh kids' with slushy snowballs.

When I remember back to my days in Caniers, some forty years ago, one memory comes to mind more than any other.

Before going into class in the morning and at lunchtime, the kids congregated in the school yard. Once the whistle blew, we formed into our respective class groups and lined up, ready to climb the iron fire escape up to the classrooms. We were always challenging each other with 'dares', and on this occasion I was in the hot seat. It was around Hallowe'en and I had brought a squib, or banger, into school. As we climbed the fire escape, towering above the rows of school kids below, I lit the banger and tossed it in the air out from the fire escape. It exploded well above the heads of the kids, their masters and the Brothers. A spontaneous cheer erupted from below.

I continued on, as if nothing had happened, with an air of angelic innocence. We entered our classroom and began our studies.

About an hour later, the door of the classroom was flung

open and in strode the burly, bull-like figure of the head brother, Brother Heron, known to us as 'Fish-face'. On this occasion, he was purple-faced with anger.

Bro. Heron had his stick, a pointer for the blackboard, grasped in one hand while repeatedly and aggressively slapping the palm of his other hand, in anticipation no doubt of administering justice to an as yet unannounced culprit.

Bro. Heron's stick was feared by all of us because it left our little palms and knuckles as purple as his face after he had trashed us for whatever failing we may have had.

I shuddered in my desk at the thought of what lay ahead.

Every kid in the class shook at the prospect on being blamed with collective responsibility for the offence. After all, it was clear that the banger had been launched from our class group, and 'Fish-face' was well known for exacting indiscriminate revenge for such mis-deeds.

'Who threw the rocket?' roared the head brother, without even bothering to excuse his unscheduled entry to our class teacher.

In the mistaken belief that honesty might be the best policy, I immediately stood up in my desk.

'I did, Brother,' said I in a quivering low voice. No one moved or uttered a syllable.

'Fish-face' seemed almost disappointed that he had got such an immediate response. He was ready to parade through the class, threatening all before him. He called out with a raspish, 'Get up here, child.'

He levelled out my shaking hands and gave me six merciless whacks on each palm with his stick. I returned to my desk, my hands numb with pain. I think I managed to keep back the tears.

Brother Heron departed and the class resumed its lesson. The teacher made no comment on either my crime or the punishment I had received.

I left my bangers at home after that.

DESMOND GUINNESS

Childhood Wear and Tears

My first memory of clothes is being dressed as a daffodil at Madam Vacani's dancing class in London, aged four. About two or three years later, I was made to sit for a head-and-shoulders portrait by Henry Lamb. When he came, I was dressed in a saffron kilt (handed down to me by my elder brother, Jonathan, now Lord Moyne) and the customary plain dark green jersey. Next day, however, I was a rhapsody in blue — blue trousers with a jersey to match. The artist was all set up to go on with my portrait and the green jersey was, of course, essential to him. I'd *never* worn it with blue trousers and was quite determined not to try. The very idea was both ludicrous and impossible and I quite naturally and rightly refused. Goodness knows how the ghastly scene ended. I can't remember.

When Jonathan and I were children, my mother often went to Germany where she attended the Nuremberg Rally on more than one occasion. It was a vast parade that was held each year on Hitler's birthday and must have been a thrilling spectacle, ending up with his birthday speech. Our mother brought back *lederhosen* for us to wear, shammy-leather trousers, embroidered, supported by a harness of punched-leather braces that were worn outside the jersey. I can remember the embarrassment of having to show off these surprise German gifts to our visitors.

Our mother also dressed us up in Nazi uniforms, both black and brown, made for children to wear, as today cowboy uniforms might be brought home by Americans from an out-of-state visit. My brother and I used to parade in these fascist uniforms down the leafy Derbyshire lanes on May Day, our ponies draped in Union Jacks and swastikas. Miss Gillies, the governess, was our only audience. If only she had had a camera!

Not long after, when I was nine, our poor mother was interned, imprisoned without trial under regulation 18B, a wartime emergency regulation. We used to visit her during the holidays from our boarding school, in the unwelcome company of a wardress; for ages we could not see her without one being present. When we gave the address of her prison to our taxi driver, he would say, 'Bit young, aren't you?'

It was not a usual childhood.

MARY HARNEY

Holiday Memories

The night before I left for a holiday, my house would seem quite different. A hall full of suitcases was testament to the fact of my plans to travel. Sleep, for me, was out of the question. I was always far too excited about going to Galway, to our relations, for our summer holiday.

On this one night of the year, I was allowed to say up late, packing and unpacking my bags, deciding what books and toys to bring, planning what I would do every day I was away. It was believed that I might wear myself out and sleep on the trip the following morning. This was a forlorn hope.

Dawn of departure day was greeted with my cries of 'Get up, it's today! Shouldn't we be going now? I'll be late arriving!'

I would spend the morning touring the house, saying good-bye to toys not thought special enough to bring and items of furniture I might not see again for two weeks.

After many rows about journey planning — 'I need a seat by the window', 'I'm not sitting beside him', 'I'm keeping my bag with me on my knee', 'What time can I have my sweets?' — we would set off. I always thought of this as a dress rehearsal. We would be back fifteen minutes later to collect something I had forgotten.

Having set off again, I would commence on travelling games. My favourite was listing, in the correct order, all the towns and villages we would pass through on the way to Galway. This feat of memory would keep me occupied for about half an hour and the end of the game signalled time for the first sweets.

Sweets, crisps and drinks of orange were vital to a successful trip. Any signs of crankiness in the back seat were treated with a sharp look from the front of the car and a liquorice Allsort. I wasn't, as a rule, fractious or troublesome on a long journey. My particular method of torment was to whine, in a high and continuing monotone, 'Are we nearly there? When are we going to get there? We must be there by now!'

And finally, sticky and stuffed with sweets, we would turn the corner into my grandmother's drive. Squealing with excitement, I would leap out of the car and start to race around the yard. Adults would disappear into the kitchen for a well-deserved cup of tea. My holiday had started.

JACK HARTE

Holidays

Holidays. First fortnight in August. The beginning and the end of every year.

Holidays had scarcely been invented for working-class people back in the fifties, yet we always went on holidays. It was simple. We had moved from the coast of Co. Sligo to the Midlands because my father's trade as a blacksmith had become obsolete. He got a job with Bord na Móna and our family settled in one of the Bord's purpose-built villages in the lovely town of

Lanesboro astride the Shannon. We felt very much at home, and secure in being only a hundred yards outside Connaught. Nevertheless, we experienced the exiles' eternal backward pull, and every summer returned to Sligo for the holidays.

From September through to the following July was one long build-up. The dreaming. The planning. The breath-stealing anticipation as the season approached.

We kept the cottage we had vacated at Killeenduff, between Easkey and Dromore West. Three bare rooms, that was all. But what more could a palace have offered? At first we travelled down by bus, the old green, chugging CIE buses that dropped boxes of day-old chicks at every second house along the way. As soon as we reached Killeenduff, we children dispersed about the countryside. Anything that moved in Tireragh, we were related to it. Cousins everywhere. Warm, hospitable people who took us in and looked after us as if we were their own, so that our parents hardly saw us from one end of the fortnight to the other.

And what did we do? The sea was half a mile away and we could swim like fish, having learned in the quieter waters of the Shannon. The bogs, the mountain, Lough Easkey, the Easkey River, all were accessible to the trundling carts on which we hitched a ride.

The family grew bigger. Eventually there were nine children. And we had a transportation problem. More things to bring. Clothes. Furniture. So we hired a lorry! Beds and chairs and tables were piled up on the back. Armchairs. Anything that might be useful. Which was everything. It was like moving house for the fortnight. Up on the back of the lorry went the children, marshalled by our mother. Squatting on mattresses, sitting on armchairs. Peering out through the crates on the side of the lorry.

As the eldest son, I was usually allowed to ride in the cab with my father. To make sure the driver didn't go astray, you know. Such responsibility at so young an age!

Those lorry journeys were the stuff of folklore. The things that happened. Once, the short-sighted driver who had come to collect us, didn't notice us, and drove past. Dozens of children. Dozens of adults. Dogs. Cats. All waving wildly at him on a deserted road along the Sligo coast. And he sailed past. My father, who was still athletic, commandeered a bicycle and chased after him, overtaking the lorry as it slowed down to negotiate the bridge at Easkey. We sighed with disappointment as the victorious cyclist led the lorry back.

Then there was the problem of my sister who suffered from habitual travel sickness. We were climbing the Curlews outside Boyle when the problem first struck. All the panic, all the desperate attempts from the back to stop the lorry, went unnoticed by the three men in the front navigating the corkscrew bends. My sister solved the problem herself; she got my wellington and spewed into it.

Times have changed. Sunshine holidays! It always rained in Sligo! Yet I dream of climbing aboard the old Ford lorry, straining for the first glimpse of Lough Arrow, holding my breath as we turn left at Ballisodare to enter Tireragh. After, all is bliss.

PAT HARTIGAN

Even though I was born in 1950 into a town-land called Drombanna which lies approximately three miles east of Limerick city, I can readily recall many natural forces that enticed me into the world of the Gaelic Athletic Association.

The 1950s was an era that brought men like the Rackards, Ring, the Doyles and many other giants of hurling into every house in Ireland. Our house was no exception. The spirit of our national game was to be found all around our immediate neighbourhood, but during the early fifties, I was too young to appreciate what the game of hurling meant and its importance to the quality of life in rural Ireland.

My longest memory takes me back to the 1959 All-Ireland hurling final between Waterford and Kilkenny. That very day gave my life a new identity as a nine-year-old lad. I can still vividly recall sitting under the kitchen table as all the neighbours gathered at our house and listened to that drawn final on a battery radio. John O'Dea, known to us as Jack Day, suggested that a cement block be put on top of the radio so that it would not jump from the table, such was the exhilarating excitement created by Michael O'Hehir through his broadcast of that game.

Fourteen years later, I was to have my hour of glory when I walked out onto that same Croke Park pitch and won, with Limerick, that same McCarthy Cup, the very one which had gripped our entire household on that famous September day in '59.

From that day forward, 'hide-and-seek' became a part of my past. The hurley and sponge ball took the place of the toy tractor and trailer. Even Santa Claus proved himself to be a very enthusiastic hurling fan for some years hence. How prophetic it was to get a pair of black and amber stockings from him that same Christmas.

Hurling was to become my bread and butter, and I was beginning to get big enough to stand in goal for 'three goals in' — a popular game with the boys in the neighbourhood. As Kilkenny's Ollie Walsh was my hero, those same black and amber stockings gave me the incentive to try and be as good as goalkeeper as he was.

From there, my hurling career progressed, first with my club, South Liberties, and then with my school, Limerick CBS in Sextons Street. It was that foundation which helped me to wear the famed green jersey of the Limerick senior hurling team for eleven years.

It was a career that filled me with unforgettable

memories until my retirement from playing the game I loved in 1980.

LIAM HAYES

The big funeral was on a Thursday morning. I had heard my dad say it was going to be a big funeral. The man was old. Forty or fifty. And he had died suddenly. The cars will be down to Swans, my dad had said. Swans was the local pub, and it was about half a mile down the hill from the church.

The church was opposite the school. I was in fifth class. It was my second year as an altar server. I was one of the old hands. Mass-serving was my business.

Funerals were as good as weddings, every bit. Better. Weddings were costly. Men at weddings knew what they were doing. Men at funerals did not care about what was in their pockets. Men at weddings had money in brown envelopes. Men at funerals dug deep into their pockets.

A funeral on a Saturday morning was work. Good work if you could get it. A funeral during school was brilliant, fantastic, the best. An hour and a half off school and getting paid for it. The best.

You could get a rusty-looking ten-shilling note at a good funeral. Split four ways. Ten-year-olds. Three or four spins down to Swans on my bike. Swans was also a shop.

The big funeral had a wooden coffin. Not brown. Not shiny. Blank wood. Everybody cried in the front rows. It was a long funeral. We would get our money, and be back in the yard by half-twelve. The funeral and a game of football. No twelve o'clock catechism. Great.

It was over. We were taking off our white and red serving stuff. Mick Mac, JJ, Rats and me. We waited. Nobody knocked on the door. Our door was down by the side of the church. At the back. Waited for ages. We heard the bell in the yard across the road. We could hear the other lads shouting.

We waited. Somebody said 'Fuck!' One 'Fuck!' We all ran out the door. We walked by all the people dressed in black. Then we ran.

It was a big funeral, I heard my dad say at tea. Down to Swans? my Mum had asked.

They must have forgotten, I thought. They forgot to pay us. They probably only remembered when they got home. They might leave the money with Father Halpin for us.

I lived next door to the priest's house. He might be in with the money tomorrow. Our boss.

PAT INGOLDSBY

Outwitting the Bogey-man

Nobody ever told me about the Bogey-man. They didn't have to. There was no official warning or anything like that. We were taught how to use a knife and fork and how to cross the road, but I can't ever remember one significant moment in my early childhood when a parent or a teacher or a garda superintendent took me gently to one side and said quietly, 'What I am about to tell you is for your own good. I have here an identikit picture — millions of children all over the world have helped us to compile it. Look at it very quickly and then look away — don't look for too long or something awful will happen — your nose will start to grow or your ears will drop off. This, my dear child, THIS IS THE BOGEY-MAN!'

We just knew. There are certain things that you know as a child without anybody ever telling you. Certain things and places. Places like 'Up in Nelly's Room behind the

Wallpaper'. You knew exactly where that was. You could even draw a map. It was a safe place. And Nelly. Nelly would never harm you. Not at all. She was more than happy to live behind the wallpaper and mind things. Things that got lost. Your mother's purse. The front door key. The tin-opener. If they went missing, everybody knew where they were. Behind the wallpaper. Up in Nelly's room.

But the Bogey-man. He was different. You knew intuitively that he was only interested in the one thing. He didn't give a hoot about lost objects. He had a sack — a personalised sack with your name on it and he couldn't rest easy until you were in it. He didn't have a wife or a mother or go to the pictures or things like that — he was much too busy monitoring *your* movements.

Me and my brother would go upstairs at night and we'd get undressed and we knew exactly how far 'grabbing distance' was from the bed — we got undressed over near the window. That was Stage One. Stage Two involved getting into bed without having your ankles grabbed.

One by one, we hurtled across the cold linoleum in our bare feet and took off like Olympic athletes bouncing up off a powerful springboard. We described a perfect arc and crash-landed onto the middle of the mattress — 'Phew! That was close!'

My brother always made me sleep on the outside of the bed. He made me lie in the high-risk area while he claimed the safe bit in against the wall.

'I'm older than you,' he said. 'When you're older, you sleep on the inside. That's . . . that's how it is.'

There was only one possible avenue of approach and that was up the outside, although as long as you kept your legs in under the covers, you were safe. The Bogey-man had this unwritten code of rules. He never grabbed your ankles when they were in under the covers. He had his own curious sense of ethics. On the one hand, it wouldn't cost him a thought to plunge you head-first into his sack, even on your birthday — it was all the one to him. Yet, at the same time, as long as you kept your legs in under the covers, you were safe. You knew the rules and so did he.

Beds in furniture shops or showrooms didn't interest him. He didn't waste his time lurking under them. Bunk beds — the top half of bunk beds — they were no use to him either. No. He much preferred to lie under mine, directly under my half, waiting patiently for me to fall asleep . . . waiting patiently for an unguarded leg.

Sometimes I would awaken in the wee small hours of the morning and the terrible realisation would creep through my body — 'Oh my God! My foot is sticking out!' But I wouldn't make any sudden movements. One sudden rash wrong move and you could be gone. Scarcely daring to breathe, I would inch my foot slowly, oh so slowly, back in under the covers . . . bit by bit . . . back into the 'No-Go' area which was covered by the rules.

I am not ashamed to admit it. I sleep on a mattress now. A mattress on the floor — with the light on. There is not a Bogey-man in the world who could work his way around that one.

JONATHAN IRWIN

Gordon Richards

It is possibly something short of obtuse to start a recollection with a passage of time that could not possibly be a shadow of one's memory.

Born as I was in England in June 1941, my mother had already taken me to Dublin by that November. Being neither cruel nor stupid, the reason she had risked the Irish Sea at the height of the U-boat war was that I was dying and there was only one man to save me. That man was Dr Colman Saunders, a name synonymous with the creation of Our Lady's Hospital for Sick Children in Crumlin.

My own first personal memory is of this Father

Christmas — the character 'Gordon Richards'. I should explain that by now, my parents had left for the war and I lived in a large house on the outskirts of a small village in Buckinghamshire. My only companion was my Austrian nurse whom we had rescued from the internment camp on the Isle of Man. She spoke little if any English, so my first language was German, which made the two of us stand out a little.

Day by day, we shopped in the village post office, I in my pushchair and she on foot, with a wild mongrel tied by rope to her waist. She would disappear through the door of the shop with the housekeeping and my pocket money, which was threepence, muttering 'Gordon Richards'. God knows what the chant meant, but it was better than 'Abracadabra!', because day after day, we would return home with an empty ration book but awash with change. By 1946, Gordon Richards had swelled my money box so much that I had bought my own tricycle. It was only then that I came to understand that Mr May, the postmaster, was an illegal bookmaker and that Gordon was a real live Santa.

JOHN B. KEANE

Far, Faint Notes

It was Christmas morning. Word had come that the door of the school, where my father was the master, was ajar. My brother Eamon, God be good to him, and myself were sent to investigate.

The school was three miles from the town, but it was a mild Christmas morning and we were young. He was twelve and I was eight. We checked the school thoroughly with the aid of a friend next door. All seemed in order. I was provided with cake and lemonade in the friend's house and Eamon was prevailed upon to partake of a small glass of sherry. I could have been prevailed upon too but I wasn't.

Later, as we neared the town we were hailed from the doorway of the tiniest house I ever saw by the proprietor. He was an expansive chap with a wife and several young children. We were prevailed upon to 'take tay'. We sang several songs and at one stage in the proceedings, there was a bit of a dance. We were asked if we would like a bite to eat, but we declined on the grounds that our own dinners would be awaiting us, that we were late as it was.

The man of the house lifted the cover from a skillet pot which hung from a crane over a warm turf fire. There emerged, accompanied by a cloud of steam, one of the most tantalising aromas we had ever experienced in our entire lives. A few local musicians arrived afterwards and we sang and danced till darkness began to fall outside.

The search party which eventually discovered us consisted of my father and another mildly inebriated teacher.

Years later, when I would meet Eamon in distant places, he would ask if the whole thing had been a dream or if such a house had ever existed. He rediscovered it shortly before he died, but it was only a ruin. His companion of the time still swears he heard the far, faint notes of a concertina.

EDDIE KEHER

For those of us who grew up in pre-television days, there is no doubt but that the greatest inspiration for us to play and try to excel in hurling was the voice of Michael O'Hehir.

Who could forget the exciting atmosphere he created in every household as he painted verbal pictures of the crowd in Croke Park on All-Ireland day? The players coming out on the pitch and parading behind the Artane Boys' Band.

The teams taking up their positions, and 'The ball is in and the game is on!'

Names like Ring, Langton, Leahy, Doyle and Rackard were left ringing in our ears as we dashed out as soon as the match was over, to relive the game on our own 'Croke Park' in the middle of the village. A match was quickly arranged as we fought over who would be 'Ring' or 'Langton'. The biggest occasion for us was when the 'Upstreets' challenged us, the 'Downstreets', to a match. These matches were arranged regularly, but not without intense negotiations and disputes! Where did the '49th parallel' lay? In other words, where did 'upstreet' start? Inevitably, we provided the venue as there was no level pitch up the hill. While they had to play 'away', we generally had to concede that the Mill Road, where a few key players lived, was 'upstreet'. Nevertheless, the greater population of youngsters lived 'downstreet' and we usually came out on top.

The recent death of Mrs Kitty White brought back a memory to me of one of the greatest of these matches. The occasion was when the 'upstreets' came to us with a proposition for a game to end all games! This was going to be the Real All-Ireland. The match, however, would have to be played at a neutral venue, and with a referee. The neutral venue was Dobbyn's field, which was half a mile outside the village, but you had to go 'upstreet' to get to it. The other major issue we were asked to accept was that Nick White (Kitty's late husband) would be the referee. He lived 'upstreet', and we would not concede here. But then they played their trump card! There would be a pre-match parade, and Nick would lead us around the field with his trumpet. (He played in the local brass band.)

How could we miss out on that! But the Mill Road lads would play with us. Agreed! Such skilful negotiators we were for eight-year-olds.

The great day came and, with the pictures Michael O'Hehir had created in our minds, we marched proudly around the field to 'Kelly, the Boy from Killane', played by

Nick, God bless him.

We lost on that day, with the help of some home town refereeing decisions (we would always contend!), but what a memory.

For some of us, the real thing came some years later, but I wonder whether it would have, but for the voice of Michael O'Hehir, the Upstreets and the Downstreets, and Nick White and the pre-match parade in Dobbyn's field.

BRENDAN KENNELLY

The Stones

Worried mothers bawled her name
To call wild children from their games.

'Nellie Mulcahy! Nellie Mulcahy!
If ye don't come home,
She'll carry ye off in her big black bag.'

Her name was fear and fear begat obedience,
But one day she made a real appearance —
A harmless hag with a bag on her back.
When the children heard, they gathered together
And in a trice were
Stalking the little weary traveller —
Ten, twenty, thirty, forty.
Numbers gave them courage
Though, had they known it,
Nellie was more timid by far,
Than the timidest there.
Once or twice, she turned to look
At the bravado-swollen pack.
Slowly the chant began —

'Nellie Mulcahy! Nellie Mulcahy!
Wicked old woman! Wicked old woman!'

One child threw a stone.
Another did likewise.
Soon the little monsters
Were furiously stoning her
Whose name was fear.
When she fell bleeding to the ground,
Whimpering like a beaten pup,
Even then they didn't give up
But pelted her like mad.

Suddenly they stopped, looked at
Each other, then at Nellie, lying
On the ground shivering.

Slowly they withdrew
One by one.

Silence, Silence.
All the stones were thrown.

Between the hedges of their guilt,
Cain-children shambled home.

Alone,
She dragged herself up,
Crying in small half-uttered moans,
Limped away across the land,
Black bag on her back,
Agony racking her bones.

Between her and the children,
Like hideous forms of fear —
The stones.

BENEDICT KIELY

The Gold Ring

One day in the 1970s in Donnybrook in Dublin, a man said to me that in fifty years, the nuns had altered out of all knowing.

'Look at that young one now,' he said, 'sprinting for a bus.'

Fair enough, on the far side of Morehampton Road, a young woman of the conventual variety was legging it along in fine style to catch a Number 10 to get out to the campus at Belfield for her university studies. The great St Teresa of Avila said that haste was the enemy of devotion, but then the great St Teresa of Avila never had to catch a bus to Belfield.

'And would you care to hear what I saw last Sunday?' the man said. 'Two of them coming out of a shop reading an English Sunday newspaper: and I remember the time when the priests used to preach against the English Sunday newspapers: and only last month there was a picture in the paper here that was an unholy show: two nuns at some class of a broadcasting conference in the Royal Dublin Society in Ballsbridge, one of them in a tweed suit and a short skirt and the other in trousers. A nun in trousers.'

To attempt to console the good man, I reminded him that one of those nuns had been American and the other from the Philippines, and it might very well be that they knew no better in those places. But, unconsoled, he left me and went on his way muttering, reminding me of one of those odd characters who used to spring to brief, enigmatic life in the meditations of Myles na gCopaleen. Didn't one of his people once say in a tone of apocalyptic warning: 'There's nothing but trousers in Russia.'

Yet that melancholy, disapproving man left me thinking his basic theory was sound enough: in fifty years, the nuns have altered out of all knowing, at any rate in outward appearance: and it is now seventy-three years since I met my first nun, two nuns to be exact, and you can take my Bible oath on it that neither of them was wearing trousers. There was Sister Patrick. There was Sister Kevin: that wasn't her real name, it wasn't even her real name in religion, but it is possible that in this world or the next, she may be around somewhere and I'm taking no chances. Sister Patrick was fat and smiling and quite incapable of harm. Sister Kevin was one tough cookie.

At the time of my first encounter with her, I had just passed my third birthday. You may be inclined to question the reliability of my observation at that time, and of my memory here and now. But there are certain things that stay in the memory forever. The desks that we sat at or in, I can see them still. The work, if that's what you would call it, that we were supposed to do. The handkerchiefs attached by safety-pins to our jerseys, the jerseys of the boys, that is, for we were co-educational. Nor, since nobody had ever heard of Freud, was our contiguity regarded as any risk to holy purity, or anything else. The handkerchiefs, so pinned onto us, were, quite literally, to hand for use and we could not easily lose them. The girls kept their handkerchiefs up their sleeves on elastic bands, nor could we ever find out how that one worked.

But the wells on my path to learning in that harem of a school were poisoned by the affair of the school reader and by the blow Sister Kevin caught me on the knuckles with her cane when I was absorbed in drawing funny faces with spittle and fingertip on the glossy, brown wooden desk.

'Wipe the desk clean this instant,' she said. 'You naughty little boy.'

You can see the reasons I had for loving Sister Kevin. She and that cane were famous. They were even in the Pancake Tuesday rhyme:

'Pancake Tuesday's a very happy day.
If we don't get our holidays we'll all run away.

Where will we run to? Up Fountain Lane,
When we see Sister Kevin coming with the cane.'

I have, often since, wondered what she had against men.
But I bested her over the business of the school reader. This
is what happened. It was a lovely school reader: sixteen
pages of simple sentences, big print, coloured pictures. It
told the most entrancing stories. This one, for instance:
'My dog, Rags, has a house. He has a little house of his
own. See, his name is over the door.'

Or this: 'Mum has made buns for tea. She has made nice
hot buns.'

Or yet another: 'When the children went to the zoo,
they liked the elephant best of all. Here is the elephant with
happy children on his back.'

That elephant I was contemplating with sombre and
scientific interest when Sister Kevin put her hand on my
school reader and said: 'Your sister tells me you have one of
these at home.'

Which was true enough. But to have one copy, which my
mother had bought me, at home and to have another copy,
supplied by regulations, in school, gave that miracle of
coloured picture and succinct narrative the added wonder
of twins and two elephants, or of having two of anything.
So when Sister Kevin, soaring to the top of her flight in the
realms of wit, said that one reader should be enough for
such a little boy, and all the female mixed-infants giggled, I
saw red and grabbed: leaving Sister Kevin speechless with
shock and turning over and over in her hand a leaf that said
on one side: ' "Here comes the aeroplane," said Tom.' And
on the other side: 'When the children came home from
town they had much to tell Mum.'

Gripping the rest of the reader, I glared at the nun who
was white in the face with something, fright or fury, at this
abrupt confrontation with the male forces of violence and
evil. She looked at me long and thoughtfully. Fortunately
for me, she was that day perambulating without benefit of

cane. She said: 'Naughty boy. Now your poor mother will have to pay for the book you destroyed. Stand in the corner under the clock with your face to the wall until hometime.'

Which I did, tearless, my face feverish with victory, because that onset with Sister Kevin had taught me things about women that some men never find out. And, staring at the brown varnished wainscoting in the corner of the room, I made my resolve: As long as I'd live, I'd never go back to that schoolful of women. I would go to the Brothers with the big boys. And I knew that my mother would create no obstacles because if I could defy Sister Kevin and live, I was more than a match for my mother. It was, I had found out, a man's world. . . .

Today, I'm not so sure. And I wonder would my world have been different if Sister Kevin had been wearing tartan slacks. There's no holy rule that says that a dainty morsel in slacks could not also be a terror with the cane on Pancake Tuesday or any other day.

At any rate, I kept my vow and crossed over to the Christian Brothers and the big boys: and my first Christian Brother was a man called Lynch, brother in the flesh to General Liam Lynch of tragic memory: and when I read Major Florry O'Donoghue's life of Liam Lynch, I found out that the first teacher the Lynch boys ever had was a man with the same name as myself and down in the southerly part of the country where the Kielys or Kileys or Na Cadhlaigh or Na Cadhla come from: a harmless coincidence meaning nothing in particular, yet one of those things that give a subtle, perhaps a magic quality to the business of living.

Thus my brief affair with the holy sister of Loreto came to an abrupt end. Somewhere in the family archives, there may be a portrait from that period. Such portraits came in inch-wide strips and six at a time. It shows, or showed, a pudgy, sullen three-year-old with untidy hair, and that handkerchief pinned to the gansey: a disgrace, I'd say, and a reproach to an elder sister, for elder sisters did not wish to be incommoded at school by little brothers or, if they were compelled to bear them company, then they treated them to a pretty sharp discipline: and the task of convoying me to the holy house of Loreto, which had once been convoyed over land and sea by angels, was given to a neighbour's daughter, May Kavanagh. May was no believer in that business about a straight line being the shortest distance between two points and to her I owe an early and sound knowledge of the geography of my home town. Had I lived longer in her company, I might have rivalled Henry the Navigator, but literature and the pictorial arts swept us apart.

From his book *Drink to the Bird: A Memoir*

BRIAN LENIHAN

My happiest childhood memories are related to sport and particularly football. I grew up in a football town, Athlone, in the 1940s, where Gaelic and soccer football were held in equal esteem, and I played both.

I was a natural right-footed player but appeared for Leinster College Gaelic football team in 1948 as left-corner forward. I started playing soccer as an outside-left, and then as centre-forward in an amateur international for Ireland in 1950.

My left foot became stronger than my right, and it was all due to a Marist brother — Brother Hubert, who insisted on me training in the old Fair Green in Athlone with a boot on my left foot and a sock on my right.

It was elementary but it made me a two-footed player. Today at the highest level, you can see the double-effectiveness of the footballer who kicks equally well with both feet.

My son Mark would have been a good footballer, but he died from leukaemia at five years of age in Our Lady's Hospital, Crumlin, in 1965. My wife Ann and I owe a great deal to Our Lady's Hospital for their loving care and treatment of Mark, who has been playing and praying for us in heaven for thirty years.

JOHNNY LOGAN

Coffin-a-go-go

We called it 'Coffin-a-go-go'. To my brothers, Michael and Eamonn, and myself, it was the most brilliant go-kart we had ever seen. Michael was the designer and driver and I was the brakeman and chief 'gofer' (go fer this, go fer that). Eamonn was also a 'gofer' but his main job was encouragement.

It was made with two six-foot planks of wood and cut in the shape of a coffin, with two sets of pram wheels (scavenged from a dump in Howth). We had a rope for steering and a piece of wood with rubber on the end for a brake. It was all held together with nails and imagination. Michael sat at the front, holding the rope which was attached to the front wheels, while I was at the back as the brakeman.

It was the day of the big race for our gang. It began half-way up the hill of Howth and was supposed to end as we turned off onto Dungriffin Road. However, if you missed the turn, the hill became so steep that you could kill yourself. There were go-karts of all shapes and sizes, but I'll always remember the one driven by little Paddy Mackey — it was a pram with rope steering.

'On your marks! Get set! Go!'

We pushed our karts as fast as we could, then hopped on

when we'd built up enough speed. The local postman must almost have had heart failure as he drove slowly down the hill in his Mini. He was overtaken by our go-karts. Imagine the look on his face as a kid in a pram passed him on the left and two heads passed him on the right. I say two heads, because Mick and myself were so close to the ground that only our heads could be seen from inside the car.

As we reached Dungriffin Road, we needed more room to turn our kart than we'd previously thought — unfortunately, that meant blocking Paddy. 'Ye b——s!' was all I heard as I watched his pram disappear up a wall and into a garden. Just then, Michael shouted at me to slow down, but as I did, our front wheels buckled and poor Coffin-a-go-go's nose hit the ground. Mick was thrown forward, bouncing along the road on his arse. He later told me that looking up, he saw me flying over him to the roar of approval from the spectators. I think you could safely say we were out of the race.

Paddy's brother, Robert, was the eventual winner of the race. All that was left for us to do was to pick ourselves and Coffin-a-go-go up and head for home. We'd have a go another day and even if we didn't, it had been great 'craic'. Even years later, Mick, Paddy and myself, and probably the postman, have never forgotten that race and Coffin-a-go-go.

SAM MCAUGHTRY

The Wild Dog Rover

In the late twenties, the depression in the city was something desperate: nearly all our menfolk were on the streets, standing at the corners unemployed, or else they were forced to work at concreting the Belfast streets on Outdoor Relief. For this they received no money — just a note that was exchanged for bare essential groceries. The Poor Law Guardians, whose idea this was, wouldn't even allow the men to draw five Woodbine cigarettes on the note, so that'll give some idea of the times that were in it.

Anyway, you can imagine how our mothers felt when Christmas time came around. There were seven surviving kids in our family, so we weren't exactly on a new bicycle each on Christmas morning. At least, anyway, the whole street was in the same boat. I got a penny and an orange in my stocking, plus a thing that unrolled and made a scraking noise when I blew it, and that was more or less what the other kids had, with two exceptions: Alec Reynolds had nothing: 'Our Rover chased Daddy Christmas back up the chimney,' he explained. We understood: his dad had been lost in the Great War. The other exception was a visitor from the country, Eddie Moore. He was staying with Mrs Jackson, his aunt, up the street, and he had more sweets in his pockets than any one of us would have eaten in a week.

When he heard Alec Reynolds's story, Eddie Moore pointed to Rover: 'Sure that thing could chase nobody anywhere,' he scoffed, and that was the signal for the whole lot of us, including Rover, to chase him the length of the street to the wee shop owned by Mrs Jackson. He ran right up the hall and hid behind her skirts:

'And what's all this on a Christmas morning?' Mrs Jackson asked.

'All I said was that Rover could never chase Daddy Christmas up the chimney,' Eddie Moore told her.

'Who owns that dog?' she asked, and we all pointed to Alec Reynolds, standing there with nothing for Christmas.

Mrs Jackson took Alec's hand, brought him into the shop, and he came out with a monster great bag of sweets. Then she bent down and lifted Rover up into her arms. He was only about six weeks old. I think he was a mongrel. 'That Rover's a wild dog,' Mrs Jackson said to Eddie Moore. 'He's ferocious. He's trained to chase people up chimneys. . . .'

From his book *Belfast Stories*

NELL McCAFFERTY

riday night was great. My father would bring home his wages in a brown envelope, sit in his armchair in the corner and open it with solemnity. We would always ask, and he would never tell us, how much he earned. 'Enough,' he would say.

This was deeply reassuring, but as I grew older, worry crept in. If there was enough, why did my mother have to go round the shops every week handing over her debt-books and a few shillings? She used to let me look at the amounts pencilled in and they were enormous. They would never be paid off. Every time the debt reduced, she'd order something else and the bill would soar again. I suggested we walk into town and save money on the bus and she laughed and repeated the story to my father and he laughed too. 'You have to enjoy yourself as well,' they'd say to me.

Sometimes, on the debt day, my mother would take me into a tea shop and order lemon pancakes sprinkled with sugar for us both. Sweet food became a symbol of stability. If my parents were poor, we'd hardly be dining like royalty downtown.

And they wouldn't be flinging money around on fish and chips, which they always did in Derry on Friday nights, which is why I loved Fridays — so did my sisters and brothers. We fought for the privilege of going to buy them. It was understood that you could open the parcel on the way home and give yourself a little snack to make up for the work of fetching them. The fish supper was wrapped in brown paper and further insulated with a sheet of newspaper. Even then, the tang of vinegar and salt seeped through and the smell would kill you with longing. You'd walk more and more slowly, holding the warm packet against your chest, sniffing and tempting yourself until you couldn't hold out any longer.

Eventually, you'd poke your finger through the wrapping

and extract a long, golden chip. I always waited until I got to the gable wall of McLaughlins' house before I did that. The heat from their coal fire came through the wall at a certain spot and you could park yourself there, your bum and chest warmed, back and front, and have a solitary, magnificent feast. It was always agony, calculating just how many chips you'd get away with taking out of the family mouth.

Eventually, there came a Friday night when my parents gave me enough pocket money to buy my own chips. This was delicious torture. How long could a person make a bag of chips last? Our gang devised a solution. We'd sit in the chipper and order a plate at a time and share them out. A plate of chips cost the same as a bag. The man who owned the place gave us one plate and six forks and let us sit in the booth as long as the money lasted. Every time the plate emptied, he'd fill it up again. I have no memory of fighting over the amount of chips consumed per person. We ate one each at a time, going round the booth in strict rotation.

In the background, adults played records on the juke-box, five for a shilling. This used to worry us too. How long would the shillings and the music last? It lasted forever. It was Friday night; they had wage-packets and money to burn. Rock and roll and Elvis Presley had just begun. Though I fell in love with everything American, I felt sorry at the same time for the Yanks. According to Elvis, 'It's Saturday night, I just got paid. . .'. Clearly, they had to work harder and longer over there before they could afford a plate of chips. I stopped worrying about my father's wages and became a happy Irish teenager.

Now I've a monthly salary and twenty years still to run on the mortgage. When the interest rate goes up, I take the bus into Dublin town, order lemon pancakes with sugar, have a bag of chips on the way home, and murmur 'Enough.' Have you noticed how very difficult it is these days to find a coal-fire-heated gable wall against which to park your bum?

TOM MCCAUGHREN

The Call of the Corncrake

It was in mid-Antrim that I spent my childhood, among fields of golden corn and blue-blossomed lint. They were summers of sunshine and winters of deep snow. Or so it seems to me now.

The corn crop was oats, and when it were tall and ripe and caressed into waves by the summer breeze, my friends and I would lie in the grass margins and listen to the call of the corncrake. Where exactly this strange bird was we couldn't tell, but its call told us it was in there somewhere. We didn't know it had come all the way from Africa to nest in our fields and rear its young, nor did we know that soon it would fly all the way back again. Indeed we seldom saw it fly at all. Even when the reaper levelled the corn, this strange bird seemed to prefer to run.

The cutting of the meadow grass for silage has left the nest of the corncrake very vulnerable, and young people nowadays will not hear its call unless they live in the west or north-west of Ireland. However, its silence reminds us that we must care for our wildlife, and if, as the poet Francis Ledwidge wrote, you hear faint voices in a dreamy noon, they will be those of other creatures.

Not that there was anything faint about one particular visitor that came all too rarely to our small stream, or burn as we called it, for a drink. No, it wasn't a bird or an animal, but a magnificent monster of clunking black iron, spinning wheels and brass. When we heard it trundling down the road, crushing a million small stones in its path, we forgot about the corncrake and made a dash for the place we knew the roadmen would be filling it up with water. There we watched with wonder as the man in oily overalls, high up at the controls, twisted and turned all sorts of knobs and handles to manoeuvre his steam-roller into position. And if, as it clunked back up the road again, we found a small piece of rubber or metal that might possibly have come off it, this became a prized possession, to be shown to all and sundry and perhaps some day bartered for something else.

It was with similar excitement that we responded to the sound of the bugle that told us the ice cream man had arrived. We immediately scurried home to plead with our mothers for our favourite coin, a brass, multi-sided threepenny or 'thruppenny' bit. The ice cream man in those days wasn't in a van, but in a red and white cart drawn by a pony. The cart was very ornate. It had, as far I recall, a roof, open sides, and the ice cream containers were set into benches between which he plied his trade. On presenting our thruppenny bit, we received what we called a slider, or wafer, and then it was off to some sunny spot again to continue idling our way through the summer holidays.

But you're probably wondering what lint is. In those days, the main crop in the North was flax, which was grown to produce linen. We called it lint. It had blue flowers, and as the linen thread was in the stem, it had to be harvested by pulling it up by the root. That was usually a wet, back-breaking job, one we left to the grown-ups. However, when the flax was being steeped in dams to rot off the outer casing, we always had other visitors. Small brown eels would come to the surface, and then it was time to get the jam jars which earlier in the year we had used for frog spawn.

By that time, the holidays were over and it was back to school. But then we had Christmas to look forward to, hopefully snow, and the joy of tracking rabbits and other things which weren't quite so elusive as the corncrake.

EUGENE McGEE

'Killing the pig' was a big event

Although my late father was a national school principal, he also engaged in a small amount of farming, which was the usual thing in rural Ireland in an age when most families tried to be as self-sufficient as possible. In keeping with this trend, for many years we bought a weaning pig. The animal was then fattened for a couple of months before being slaughtered to provide bacon for the family for the following twelve months. In those days, however, we did not slaughter pigs — we killed them.

'Killing the pig' was a great occasion in the life of most families in my part of north Longford in the fifties and early sixties. Because it was an event that only took place once a year, there was always an eager sense of anticipation and as the time drew near, a festive atmosphere developed in the family, or at least among the children. The strange thing was that the pig would have become virtually a pet with us during the time he was being fattened up, but we never regarded his imminent demise as a cause of sorrow at all. It was seen as quite natural that a pig would be killed to provide bacon for the household.

Only one man could kill a pig in our area. Paddy Reilly, who lived just down the road, was also the only person to cut our hair, inject cattle for blackleg and do various farmyard chores.

A few days before the event, a big shed would be cleaned up and a wooden bench would be scrubbed up. Because of my father's occupation, our pig-killing tended to be during school holidays. Early in the morning, a couple of neighbours would be rounded up to help Paddy Reilly, and the actual slaughtering of the pig was carried out very expeditiously, although we children were never allowed to be involved.

We were only allowed into the shed when the recently-deceased pig had been hung up by the hind legs from a high beam and the carcass had been gutted and cleaned to a spotless condition with boiling water. We could watch the subsequent 'butchering' of the animal, and this whetted our appetites for the sumptuous goodies we knew would be on the menu later that day and for several days afterwards. We used the word 'griosgeens' for the tasty pieces of edible offal which were extracted from the pig. Hardly anything was thrown away and my mother would recycle offal into the tastiest of dishes.

For us boys, however, the big prize was the pig's bladder. After it was dried out, it could be inflated to the size of a football and it served in that capacity for days afterwards. The 'owner' of the pig's bladder had a greatly inflated status with his peers for the duration of the new-fangled football. Meanwhile, the process of preserving the bacon got under way, with hams wrapped in gauze and hanging up over the kitchen fire where they would probably remain until the following Christmas.

'Killing the pig' in the manner of my childhood days would get very short shrift from the politically correct world we live in today; EU health officials might not be too keen on it either. But it never did us any harm and the event helped to brighten our lives in those pre-television/video/computer days.

Martin McGuinness

Courage

When I was eleven years old, I nearly died. Well, that's what they told me. A burst, or to use the correct medical term, perforated appendix was the cause of my spending six whole weeks in Altnagelvin Hospital in Derry.

Awakening from the anaesthetic, it is debatable whether being told that I could have died concerned me more than the thought of being unable to play football at Teasie Coyle's gable wall. Coming as I did from a Gaelic- and soccer-mad football family, I made my decision. Football, as Bill Shankly said, is not a matter of life or death — it's far more serious than that.

When you are eleven years old, death is a stranger. Relieved not to have made its acquaintance, I quickly decided that I'd be as well persevering with hospital treatment and the rubber tubes which, in an intruding and protruding kind of way, were draining the poison from my stomach.

'How long do you have to stay in hospital when you've had your appendix out?' I asked a more seasoned inmate.

'Oh, about a week to ten days,' came the reply.

'Not too bad,' I thought to myself.

'Not too bad' changed to despair when informed by the doctor that a burst appendix required a six-week stay in hospital. Even my anguished wail — 'Oh, God! This is going to kill me!' — made no impression whatsoever on the smiling doctor. Seeing the funny side of it, I grudgingly came to terms with an injured footballer's predicament.

It soon became clear to me that the very serious and determined attempt made by doctors and nurses to restore me to full physical health was accompanied by an assault on my mental well-being. Boredom was a new and destructive enemy which had to be defeated at all costs. Night time was the worst. My yearning for freedom increased each time I shuffled to the huge window at the end of the ward where I stood wistfully gazing across the Foyle valley to Derry's West Bank and the winking, welcoming lights of Creggan. After an hour or so as a heartbroken exile, I caught myself on. Yearning and moaning gets you nowhere, I concluded.

'Do something!' I instructed myself. 'Do something! Try for a date with a nurse, read, attempt an escape — the laundry basket, perhaps? — Get to know the other patients, climb up onto the roof and maybe, just maybe, catch a glimpse of a match a mile away as the crow flies at the Brandywell Stadium or Celtic Park.'

Desperation being the real mother of invention, after five minutes of that I tried a new tack and circled the other patients. I decided to adopt the direct and diplomatic approach.

'What's wrong with you, then?' I asked.

Leonard O'Donnell, a healthy-looking young Donegal man of around twenty, replied, 'Sore back.'

An elderly Derryman named Charlie McLaughlin jokingly said, 'Old age!'

'Mind your own business!' barked a less affable soul.

Another refusenik answered my question with another, 'What do you want to know for?'

When you're eleven years old, a range of replies like these is almost as bewildering as the British government's approach to the peace process. Even then, I preferred humour and directness to evasiveness or hostility. Charlie McLaughlin and Leonard O'Donnell became my friends in hospital. There is an old saying in Irish, Giorraíonn beirt bóthar — 'Two shorten the road'. Well, Charlie and Leonard certainly did. I resigned myself to a lengthy stay and with their help made the best of it, the whole while looking forward to going home to my family.

The time to leave Altnagelvin soon came. I said good-bye to my two new-found friends and rejoined the world outside the window. Four weeks after my release from hospital, Leonard O'Donnell died from cancer. Sore back, indeed! Thirty years later, I've never forgotten him.

JOHN MACKENNA

Whatever about the warmth of childhood summers and the blueness of the skies, the excitement of Christmas was unmatched, for me, by any other time of the year. The decorations never went up in our house until Christmas Eve. The cooking had been done, the big shopping trip to Athy had taken place the previous Saturday and now, on the afternoon of Christmas Eve, it was time to put up the decorations.

The old enamel bucket was resurrected from the coal-shed and covered in red crepe paper. The sweet-smelling tree was man-handled through the kitchen and put standing in the bucket, anchored by stones and logs until, at last, it stood straight. Then the decoration began — tinsel, baubles, the silver star and lights. The lights that never lit. Pat Behan or Michael Hunt arrived and gave them their annual overhaul and there was light!

By now my aunt had arrived, driving in from the Midlands. I traipsed up and down the village a dozen times — more milk, cartons of cream, an extra loaf ('You'd never know who'd call'), late cards that would arrive in the New Year, the ham from Copes.

As Mrs Whelan rang the Angelus from the other end of Keatley's field, we lit the candle in the window and put the infant in the crib. But always, always, there was something that had been forgotten. A last, out-of-breath scurry to catch some shop before it closed. Running home, I watched the night sky apprehensively. This was not a night to be caught out late.

'Don't be silly,' my sister said. 'He hasn't left the North Pole yet.'

And, sure enough, there he was on the radio, reading a few last letters before setting off. Once, I remember, I heard my name but that wasn't important — named or not, he would come to our house. I willed myself to sleep. Was that the ring of jingling bells on the slates?

And then sleep and waking.

Down, apprehensively, to the sitting room. Maybe he's still there. No, he's come and look at this!

The rest of that day was a sack filled with smells and tastes and surprises and, finally, with tiredness.

St Stephen's morning contained as much promise as the day before. The early sleeping house, the half-full box of Black Magic, Lemon's sweets spilled under the sofa, a breakfast of trifle because no one was looking and, after lunch, the matinee. Peter Murphy at the door, Frank MacDonald trying, vainly, to keep us cowboys in our seats. Prizes for everyone and then out into the dark afternoon, guns blazing, home to games of 'twenty-five', cold turkey, hot pudding and lemon sauce.

Later, the snow came but that was a new year, as far removed from Christmas as it could be. It had nothing to do with the absolute wonder, the complete belief, the reality of Santa Claus, the knowledge that in the night of Christmas, as our candle stayed burning, the infant Christ did pass, did smile, did feel his heart warmed by the welcome we had made for him.

I've lost many things in the years since then, but never the real wonder and excitement of those Christmases. They've never sunk beneath the waves of cynicism. They're moments I treasure and hope I never lose.

BARBARA MCMAHON

When I was about six years old, had long curly hair, blue eyes and a permanent smile on my face (in fact because I was made of sugar and spice and all things nice), I was a little joy.

My brother Paul is fifteen months older than me, and at that stage that made him seven-and-a-quarter. He didn't have grey hair then, nor was he two stone overweight. Nevertheless he was made of rats and snails and puppy dogs' tails — and he was my hero.

But the feeling wasn't mutual. I used to trail around behind him and his friends like a shadow as they caught tadpoles in jam jars, climbed trees for birds' eggs and dissected dead field mice.

Just because I wore pretty gingham dresses with bows in my hair and patent-leather shoes, they wouldn't accept me into their group. Well, I suppose the real reason was because I was a *girl*.

I used to lie awake at night wondering what I could do about this. I could change my clothes and put on shorts and a tee-shirt. I could get dirty and not wash. I could get cut and scratched by brambles and not cry, but there really wasn't a lot I could do about being a *girl*.

However, I decided to give myself a make-over. (Maybe this is where 'Head 2 Toe' all started.) The clothes were easy. I found a pair of Paul's khaki shorts and a shirt that fitted perfectly, so I thought that if I wore these, nobody would know whether I was a girl or a boy — except for the hair. The two plaits just had to go.

So with the blunt kitchen scissors, I cut off each plait as close to the roots as possible, leaving me with a style that resembled a badly-plucked chicken. But I certainly looked much more like a boy. As I admired my work in the mirror, the bedroom door opened. It was my mother coming to tuck me in.

To this day, I can still see the look of horror on her face as she picked up the plaits from the floor. Words were beyond her, but I knew I was in for it.

I got no pocket money for six weeks, was sent to bed early for a month, and my birthday party was cancelled.

But the good bit was that Paul and his friends thought I

was so brave to do what I had done. Because I had proved my worth as a true tom-boy, they allowed me to become an honorary member of the gang . . . for life!

BRYAN MACMAHON

The Monster

Four years of age. Back that way, they told me, lived the Monster. He'd choke you quick as wink. He dressed in bluey-green trimmed with white. Roaring sometimes, laughing other times.

'When will I see the Monster?'

'Wait for the fine day,' Mommaw said.

Summer came. I got a painted bucket and a small shovel. Put on my sailor's suit with 'HMS *Intrepid*' on the cap. 'I'm off to fight the Monster,' I told everyone.

A queer train! Like a long donkey with turf baskets. Puff-puff — off went the train. With me and Mommaw in it.

The road ran beside the track. A pony and trap raced our train. We won. I waved my cap: it fell out the window. 'Doubt you,' Mommaw said.

At last we stopped. Everyone got out. The air smelled like bacon and cabbage. People on verandas like cups on a dresser. A piper snored a tune. Periwinkles and sea-grass on carts. A lawn. Men hitting a timber ball with mallets. 'Pock-pock,' said the tennis ball.

Next came a broken castle on a cliff. Behind it lived the Monster. I gripped Mommaw's hand.

Oh! The Monster was the sea! It stretched away away. All green ink. A lot of builder's sand. I dug a wet part. My shovel broke. I bawled. I fell into a pool under the cliff. My suit was drenched. 'Doubt you,' my mother said.

She stripped me. Spread my suit out in the sun. 'He's too

young for togs,' she said. Her swimsuit was bulgy. She walked me to the water. 'I'm not going in there,' I wailed. Mommaw caught me like this. Dashed me down into a huge wave. I swallowed water. I bawled and ran for the sand. 'She thrun me down,' I wailed at two old women who questioned me.

Then I ate sandwiches with real sand in them. My legs were goldy with sticky grains of sand. I had lemonade in Shortis' parlour. I ate sweets and turn-up in the yard.

At the station, Mommaw spoke to Jackie, the engine driver. 'Stop near Walshes',' she said, 'this fellah lost his cap.'

The train stopped. No station, only fields. A girl ran along the line waving 'HMS *Intrepid*'.

'That's mine!' I shouted.

Mommaw gave the girl a shilling. She gave me nothing. Only tried to drown me in 'the Monster'.

TOM MACSWEENEY

I remember one dark, cold morning in the fifties — a confused child's recollections of the kitchen in our home at Montenotte on the hills above Cork city. A morning of hustle and bustle, but with a sadness and upset that left me with a memory of uncertainty and doubt that the grandparents I lived with at the time did not seem to be able to control all aspects of life. In the kitchen that morning, something was happening which badly affected them and the security I was used to.

There weren't too many cars about in those days, not even in the Montenotte which was considered a 'better side' of the city. But the hired car came to the door and, somewhere within my memory, I heard a radio and the eight o'clock news. Then we got into the car and the man who was the focus of attention was being consoled as we drove off. Our destination was Penrose Quay — from where the ship departed for Britain. This was my first experience of emigration and that morning has been dug from the recesses of my mind, as a few of my experiences of life since coalesce in that occasion — unemployment, emigration, a quayside and a ship.

That was the occasion when the first member of the family, a close cousin, had to leave because there was no work in his home city. It was also the start of the big trek of unemployed people from Cork who went to Dagenham to work in the Ford factory there.

Years later, in the eighties, when the Ford car assembly plant in Cork closed down, the memory of men leaving for Dagenham came to me again. There has been many a factory closure in the Cork area since then and many a Corkonian has had to leave the city to seek work elsewhere. The shipping concentration in the city centre has also moved down-river to a big new deep-water port at Ringaskiddy, though some smaller vessels still come to the city quays; I have even sailed up to there myself.

But somewhere, my childhood memories created an atmosphere which has taken me into the special interest of the marine sphere, much neglected in Ireland. I now have two sons with deep-sea international shipping companies who sail the world's oceans and are experienced visitors all over the world.

My childhood memories of Cork also recall walking with my grandfather through the lanes and streets on the hills of Cork, areas where he could recall the history of the city to a child's wondering ears, mixed amidst the bells of the city's churches calling the faithful on Sunday mornings, which was when he liked to walk through the city.

That time of the week is still special for me on Leeside. The crowded, busy hustle of the commercial weekday life is not there and those of us who love a city can enjoy it, even if it is temporarily a city without many people.

But it is people, after all, who make a city, and even those who have had to leave it can still recall what it means for them. From that dark morning in the fifties, which I recall, I can still hear the voices of the city's dockers, preparing a crowded ship to leave for Britain — long before the comfortable days of car ferries — voices which, while engaged in their own work to get the ship away, could still express the sorrow of a Corkonian when a fellow Leesider had to leave. . . ''Tis a shame we can't have enough work for you here. . .' Not a lot has changed in many years in some regards.

DES MAGUIRE

The Fastest Gun Alive

We were twelve years old and deadly enemies. Day after day, we glowered at each other across the turf-plots of the Bog of Allen as our fathers cut the slushy peat. If looks could kill, we were both dead men.

It was our job to catch the wet sods in mid-air as they came hurtling from the *sléans*, to stack them neatly on the wooden bogeys, and when these were filled, to lead the ass out onto the cut-away where the turf would be left for the first drying. The only trouble was, he was able to tip his bogey over to dump the sods, and I wasn't!

Oh, how he sneered at me every time he made a return journey for another bogey-load of freshly-cut turf, while I had to wait submissively and patiently for my father to jump down from the bank and to follow me up the cut-away to tip the loads. The sheer humiliation of it all! His was the kind of sneer that Broderick Crawford used to torment Glenn Ford with in *The Fastest Gun Alive*; the kind of sneer no decent man deserved — the kind that stayed in

118

your memory for days, if not weeks, afterwards.

But what could I do to wipe it off his face? I knew that he wasn't any stronger than me because we both played football together in Newbridge and had clashed on numerous occasions. Yet try as I might, there was no way I could tip over that bogey, while he was able to flick it over effortlessly, if not contemptuously.

Then one day, my father walked out with me as I led the ass to the headland. He had decided to call it quits for the day and that's why he decided to accompany me.

'It's time you started tipping over that bogey yourself,' he chided. 'Let me see you having a go.'

I groaned and groaned as I tried to tip the bogey from under its flat board but there was no way it would budge. I knew my twelve-year-old rival was watching my efforts intently from his own plot and I could almost feel the heat of his sneer on the back of my neck.

'Good God, man,' said my father, 'have you not been pulling up the chain to give yourself some slack to turn the bogey over? Charles Atlas himself wouldn't turn it over like that.'

He pulled the chain and yoke up closer to the ass's legs, and said, 'There, have a go now.'

I bent down, hands firmly gripped under the board of the bogey, and almost tossed the ass over as well as the truck. The load seemed to be as light as a feather, once you had the knack and weren't trying to fight against a strained chain as well.

A few evenings later when we were playing football on the school pitch, I went hard, but fair, into my 'old enemy' and left him stretched out on the ground.

As he gazed up at me, he could see my eyes grinning at him, if not my mouth. It was the kind of grin that Glenn Ford had in his eyes as he peered down into the grave where Broderick Crawford lay at the end of *The Fastest Gun Alive*!

MARTIN MANSERGH

Coming Home to Tipperary in the 1950s

My father, Nicholas Mansergh, was born at home and remained all his life the youngest pupil at the old Abbey School in Tipperary. He was a historian and spent most of his adult life teaching and writing on Irish history and Commonwealth affairs. While my eldest brother was born in the Rotunda in January 1941 (where my mother was prescribed Guinness to encourage lactation), my brothers and sisters and I were born and mainly brought up across the water. But every summer during the long vacation, we came home to Friarsfield, two miles outside Tipperary town, where my grandmother lived and my father owned a farm. Later as we became older, we came with enthusiasm at Christmas and Easter as well. My Uncle Gregor, Aunt Marjorie and my first cousin Philippa lived up the road at Grenane, an early eighteenth-century house on the family demesne. Each September, as we left, my grandmother gave us each five pounds, and my uncle marked our height in pencil against the edge of the drawing-room door and wrote in the year.

On arrival in Dublin from Liverpool, it took some hours for the car to be hoisted off the boat, time to visit Grafton or O'Connell Street and climb Nelson's Pillar. I can still vividly recall the sounds of the horses and carts on the cobbled quays across from the North Wall, and admiring the Guinness train at Kingsbridge Station. There was a genteel shabbiness about Dublin in the 1950s. I first really got to know it when I stayed with my grandmother at the old Standard Hotel in Harcourt Street in 1961 and 1962 for a few days before Easter. On our way down to Tipperary in a heavily overladen car, four children squeezed in the back and one in the front, we always seemed to break down or get a puncture on the bad stretch of road between Kildare and Monasterevan.

The long, warm summers in the Irish countryside, with a view from the house over the fields to the Galtee Mountains, were an idyllic contrast to suburban England. There was a sense of space and freedom in which to play and roam. The farm was a busy place, with several men employed. There were hens, chickens and pigs in the yard, a Shorthorn dairy herd (the fresh, warm milk straight from a TB-tested cow was delicious), and cattle, sheep and oats down the fields. Every morning as a small child, I took a ride with the donkey and cart and the herdsman, Henry Kiely, a mile to the creamery where the waiting queue facilitated a natural social life. We also enjoyed rides up from the hayfield and an occasional visit to the market to watch how bargains were made and differences split.

The farm was managed for my father by Mr Denis McGrath, an auctioneer, who was active in the old IRA and enormously respected in the locality. He was a fount of wisdom and experience to a young boy like myself.

I was acquainted with 'the other tradition' in England, as I had a Presbyterian nanny, a Miss Eleanor McClenaghan from Portmagee in the North of Ireland, who was a marvellous friend in every way. But the reaction which her mild anti-popery created inoculated me at an early age from sectarian prejudice. All the same, she told me of the horror of Cromwell's sack of Drogheda, in total contrast to the heroic role attributed to him in the English school history books.

On Fridays, boots were needed in Tipperary town, with the market held on the Main Street, until the shopkeepers succeeded in banishing cattle and trucks to market yards. In those days, before provincial towns were as well stocked as they are today, we drove to Limerick on shopping expeditions, the only place for books and records.

In the 1950s, the local roads around Tipperary were dusty and untarred. At the age of ten, I was allowed to go on long thirty-mile bicycle rides to Lisvernane and through the Glen of Aherlow to Galbally and back, the only hazards being dogs, not traffic. There was often water rationing at home, since we were dependent on the rain-collecting tank above the roof. Water was heated in small cylinders above the basin, and drinking water had to be drawn from the pump in the yard. The bath water was severely rationed. Summers were drier and droughts more frequent in those days. The telephone had a handle to it, which had to be turned vigorously to get the local exchange. The house had a warren of pantries, good for hide-and-seek. We played cricket or clock golf on the front lawn.

My grandmother was a cultivated woman. She would sit on the bench outside the front door, knitting pullovers for her grandchildren. Thirty years on, I still very occasionally wear a black one she knitted for me. I spent a lot of time talking to her about the past. She was a fount of knowledge on family history and local families. Every week, Cousin Cass would come and visit her, as would, from time to time, old Mrs Johnstone, widow of a Church of Ireland canon, and sometimes Dolly Sadlier and her sister. Little though I knew it, a social world was finally passing away. Of about sixty-six landed families who served on the Tipperary Grand Jury in the early 1830s, only about half a dozen remain in situ today.

My father was a very good tennis player. He gave us, and the children of members of a similar age, coaching every Tuesday at the Co. Tipperary Lawn Tennis Club, which my Uncle Gregor ran with others for close on fifty years. There I made many good friends of my own age from different religious backgrounds. At the annual Munster hardcourt championships, I watched or encountered some of the country's best tennis players. It was exciting to watch my mother, who was keenly competitive, play in the finals of the ladies' singles several years running, as well as in the ladies' doubles with my father. One exceptional year, she won all three events. In winter and early spring, we sometimes followed the hunt from Grenane or went to the point-to-point of the Black and Tan Hunt at Knocklong, scene in 1920 of a famous rescue of a prisoner by Sean Treacy and his comrades.

On fine August days, we would often take off for the sea — Stradbally, Dunmore East or Ardmore — with high tea at the Cliff Hotel. As dusk fell, we liked to drive back up the beautiful Blackwater Valley to Lismore or Cappoquin, past Mount Melleray with its monks vowed to silence, and over the Vee with the chequered vale lying before us.

Other times, we went west for the Atlantic breakers at Ballybunion or Lahinch. A special treat was stopping off at Shannon Airport on the way back for mixed grill at the restaurant and to watch the planes. I remember being taken to Bunratty Castle when it was first opened. It was fairly bare, compared with today. The Rock of Cashel was great fun, as we could climb up all the staircases to the open roof, before people worried about insurance claims.

My father had a great sense of place, and he told us the historical associations of everywhere we passed — the Liberator's house in Derrynane; Parnell's last despairing fling of his arms in College Green as a dying man in 1891; Smith O'Brien's friendship with his great-grandfather, Richard Southcote Mansergh; the ambush site at Sologheadbeg; the spot on the Knockmealdowns where Liam Lynch died; Father Matthew's statue near the ruins of Thomastown Castle.

As children, we got on very well with my grandmother's cook, Breda, and later Margaret Ryan, as well as with the men working on the farm and some of the neighbours who used to call up regularly to talk to my father, people like Denis Heffernan and Paddy Guinan. Through them, as well as through my father, uncle and grandmother, I must have picked up quite a lot of the ways of the Irish countryside. There was great poverty forty years ago, children going about without shoes, large families living in one or two bedrooms, old women wearing the traditional black shawl.

At St Faith's School in Cambridge, one of the teachers

gave me the nickname 'Bogbean', which from the other side also helped to create a sense of identity. As Parnell discovered in Cambridge, and eighteenth-century Irish gentlemen before him and Loyalists since, no matter what the religious or social background, to the English, anyone from Ireland or with Irish roots was liable to be regarded, affectionately or otherwise, as a person associated with bogs. I laughed when I first came across, in Maria Edgeworth's *Castle Rackrent*, the attachment to the same bit of bog that had been in the family for hundreds of years, even though the part of Tipperary I come from is as fertile as one could wish.

While there was respect for the family in Tipperary, I also sensed a silent expectation that some member or members of my branch of the family would come home for good. In my late teens, I remember an ITGWU official, who sold books and postcards below the Rock of Cashel, saying to me, 'Of course, you'll stay. . .' or words to that effect. As a descendant of a minor landowning family which had lived comparatively well off the land, though not free of financial problems, in Cork and Tipperary for around 300 years, I felt, growing into adulthood, as I am sure my father felt, that I had a duty to give something back.

The Ireland of the 1960s was forging ahead in an exciting manner. I wanted, if possible, to find the opportunity to take part, even though my social background and largely English upbringing might be more of a disadvantage than an advantage. Both my brother, who is a planner in Cork, and I, who initially joined the Department of Foreign Affairs, were given that opportunity. The meeting point of the extended family is still Tipperary, which I try to get to as often as possible at the weekend. My youngest daughter Harriet still plays at weekends with her second cousin, Serena, where we played with her mother Phillipa thirty-five to forty years ago.

MAXI

The strains of 'Gilly Gilly Ossenfeffer Katzenellen Bogen by the Sea' were filling the Ford as Dad and I drove along that Saturday. Dad looked really handsome as the sun glinted on the driver's window. He was, in my nine-year-old opinion, the splitting image of Henry Fonda in his prime, and Mum like Grace Kelly in hers. Was I lucky or what?

Dad was an insurance agent. He collected money door to door. It was precious money, carefully saved by his clients, to ensure a safe and honourable burial or a little something to have for family milestones.

He was a familiar and well-loved figure. A great time-keeper. He'd tell us again and again as children how important it was to keep time. He'd give me lots of important grown-up tips like that as we shared our time together. We'd talk about really important things, like the latest adventures of Curly Wee or Rusty Reilly in the evening papers, in between our times of singing along to the radio. I'd open the window and the air would blow through the car and, in as loud a voice as we could manage, the strains of 'Big Rock Candy Mountain' or 'The Happy Wanderer' would lift the spirits of all who heard. Great fun!

Dad averaged about seven minutes a call. We'd time it. He'd make up the time or lose it, depending on happy or sad news at each house. He'd say, 'Good morning, Mrs Weir,' and tip his hat. 'Ah, good morning, Mr Mac,' would come the reply. In school I became known as Miss MacC, later to be shortened to Maxi. The money would be checked, the book marked, and a tip of the hat again would signify the end of the encounter until the exact same time the following week.

I was painfully shy as a child. My parents never referred to it, but I knew they knew. That afternoon, it was the farthest thing from my mind. There was a short journey to the next call, so Dad started 'Ten Green Bottles'. I was happily singing about five being left when he pulled the car gently to the kerb.

'Do the next call,' he said, out of the blue. I froze.

'Me?' I asked, shocked.

'It's Mrs Lyons,' he said, matter of factly. 'She's due to pay six shillings and eight pence. You count the money, mark it paid in the book she'll have on the hall table and write your initials in the left-hand column. Clear?'

I felt my guts twist in panic. 'Why me?', I said. 'D-D-Dad! W-why me?'

''Cos you can do it, and I need your help,' came the lilting reply.

'I c-c-can't,' I stammered.

'Up to yourself,' the soft blue eyes looked straight past me. 'But if you help me out now, I might go home through Templeogue. . . up to yourself. . . .'

Going home through Templeogue meant a stop at Patchetti's, and a stop at Patchetti's meant the tastiest ice cream in the world. Italian ice cream, Italian cones, Italian servings!

That hit home.

I looked out the window. Mrs Lyons was standing in her garden, feeding hot scones over the wall to her kids and the neighbours' kids as they argued over whose turn it was to play hopscotch.

'What do I have to do?' I whispered, tasting the ice cream in my mind, a portion of which resembled a football.

'Okay,' said the man with the determination and the delightful northern accent. 'Say hello, take the money, mark the book, say thank you and good-bye, see you next week.'

'Mark the book!' I blubbered. 'I can't!'

'You can!' The gentle voice reassured me. 'You can do anything you put your mind to, once you believe you can.'

All of a sudden, I knew I could. All of a sudden, I wasn't just a nine-year-old, afraid of everything. I was Mr Mac's daughter, with an important assignment. If I didn't do this now, the ice cream shop would be closed.

'Afternoon, Mrs Lyons,' says I, full of business. 'The total is six shillings and eight pence.'

'I have it ready,' says she, with a knowing look at Dad.

'Wonderful,' says I, all biz. 'Nice day, isn't it?' I checked the money, updated the book, sealed the information and turned to go.

My little legs were shaking as I walked slowly back to the car. Dad's grin was the size of the Phoenix Park.

'Dad!' I shouted. 'Dad! I did it! I did it! I did it!'

'All on your own,' says he, proud as punch. 'Sure, no bother to you. Aren't you Mr Mac's daughter?'

I never forgot that moment.

Years later, as I stood on the dark stage of the Gaiety one afternoon and auditioned for a three-girl group, I thought of the courage Dad had instilled.

Months after that, when that group had become 'Maxi, Dick 'n Twink' and we auditioned for 'Opportunity Knocks', I remembered the positive, positive words which Dad had taken the time to whisper to a terrified, shy, young girl.

I remembered them later again, when I auditioned for a song in the National Song Contest and ended up representing my country. And later still, when I auditioned for the group 'Sheeba', and especially the day I was fighting for my life after a car crash which ended the singing careers of those three musical ladies — and I awoke to hear the ambulance driver whisper an act of contrition into my ear with the words, 'I don't think this one will make it. . .' — I found the courage somewhere to get well, so that I could look into the faces of my mum and dad and say, 'I DID IT!'

And especially the night in Lebanon when I was asked to sing a song to cheer our soldiers on overseas duty. With the fighting in Tyre and Sidon echoing in our ears, we all joined in. On my way back to base in the AML90, the soldier driving us said, 'Hey, I felt the tears in my eyes tonight, Max. . . You're Mr Mac's daughter, aren't you?'

JAMES MOLYNEAUX

At the age of eleven, I was walking home from school when I met seven taxis conveying wedding guests to the local church. A wheel detached itself from the rear axle of the third vehicle — one vehicle passed me on one side and the disabled taxi on the other.

This, for a young schoolboy, was quite exciting. The suspension of the speeding taxi soon collapsed onto the rough road surface, making a noise which had to compete with the screams of the six lady passengers who were ushered to Mrs Murphy's pub, where some form of liquid sedative was prescribed and administered.

After half an hour, the patients emerged in all their wedding finery and with spirits greatly uplifted.

KEVIN MORAN

One of the best days of my school life was the day we won the schools' hurling final at Croke Park. My school was James's Street CBS primary school and I was eleven years old. All of us in the team were all very excited at the thought of playing at Croke Park in front of such a large crowd. We could talk of nothing else for weeks, much to the annoyance of some of our teachers!

Finally the big day arrived. Five double-decker buses pulled up outside the school and the team, all the teachers and the rest of our friends piled in, all singing and shouting. We were off!

When we got to Croke Park, myself and the rest of the team were brought to the dressing room. We were very nervous but really excited. The time seemed to flash by and suddenly it was time to run out onto the pitch. It was huge and I can remember suddenly feeling very small. The referee blew his whistle and with a big roar from the crowd, the game began.

We played fast and furiously and everything seemed very hazy, like we were in a bubble. The yells from the crowd seemed far away and all that mattered was getting vital points. Slowly the score inched up, first our team, then the other. It was a race against time. Suddenly the final whistle blew loudly. It was all over and we had won by a few points. The crowd went mad and we were all jumping up and down. We couldn't believe that we had done it.

Triumphantly, we clattered our way back to the big dressing room to get changed. Suddenly, all the elation was too much for me and I sat down on the bench with my hands on my knees. As the others quickly made their way into the room next door for the celebration party, I was left alone, still wearing my kit. One small tear trickled down my face, then another, and another, until I was sobbing my heart out. I was so happy! I could hear the shouts and laughter next door as someone burst a balloon. I wanted to go in but I couldn't stop crying. Finally, the door opened and my dad came in to look for me. I slowly stopped crying and when I was calm, still sniffing, dad brought me in to the party. It was great!

Afterwards, we all piled back into our double-deckers, singing 'We are the champions'. The bus drivers circled the area around our houses, dropping us all off. They blared the bus horns and we all yelled like mad. When we got to my house, all the neighbours were out, clapping and cheering. I got off the bus and was surrounded by everyone slapping me on the back, saying 'Well done'. Inside the house, there was a special tea laid out and I was the guest of honour. I told the story of the day again and again, remembering new things each time.

Way past my normal bedtime, I finally made my way

upstairs. For ages, I couldn't sleep but eventually I did, drifting off with the biggest smile on my face. That was a fantastic day!

PADDY MORIARTY

The Shoe

When I was young, the summers were magical times. Every July, when school broke for the holidays, I would head off with my mother and sisters to my mother's home place just outside Killarney. Six weeks in Co. Kerry each year left me with many childhood memories, and 1961 was no exception. My abiding memory from that holiday was a trip to Dublin for the Down vs Kerry All-Ireland senior football semi-final in August.

There was great excitement that Sunday morning. My Uncle Mick, God rest him, took me and some friends to Dublin as a special treat, my first ever visit to Croke Park. Down were reigning All-Ireland champions and with Kerry still smarting from their defeat by Down the previous September, interest in the game was very high, so high, in fact, that far more people assembled at Killarney railway station than CIE could cope with. There were hundreds there, men, women and children. It seemed as if everyone in Kerry was travelling to Dublin. Children had to sit on adults' knees and it was a great thrill to sit on the knee of Dee Connor, a legendary Kerry footballer from the Kingdom's first four-in-a-row winning team. The train travelled so slowly that at Mallow a second one was provided.

The game itself is now just a blur. I was only nine years old at the time, but an incident which happened on the journey home will be remembered for the rest of my life. My uncle and our party were joined in a compartment by a man from Killarney town, who shall remain nameless. This man had taken Kerry's second championship defeat at the hands of Down particularly badly and his sorrows had been well and truly drowned.

As the train sped southwards through the plains of Co. Kildare, there was a great banter. My uncle knew this man very well and we were having great crack. Despite the result, my friends and I were still very excited with our day out. I remember that it was very warm in the carriage and our friend, in need of some cool air, opened the window in the door the whole way down. He was teasing us youngsters and I recall how he grabbed my shoe and pulled it off my foot. The memory is vivid. For a few miles, he pretended he was going to throw my shoe out the open window. I tried unsuccessfully to grab it back, but each time he would move his arm as if to throw. My heart was in my mouth.

Finally disaster struck. The shoe slipped from his hand. I can still see it hurtling through the air and out the window. I nearly died and didn't know whether to laugh or cry. What was I going to say when I got home? My uncle assured me that everything would be all right. That made me feel much better. Before long, I saw the funny side of what had happened and we all had a good laugh.

Like all good stories, this one had a happy ending. The following morning, our 'friend' arrived at my uncle's home and insisted on taking me to Killarney to buy me a new pair of shoes.

LOUISE MORRISSEY

I remember our 'old house', where we lived until I was four years old. My youngest brother was only six weeks old when we moved to our 'new house', just next door.

I can remember having lots of fun with my older brothers and sisters in the old house. There was a big tree in the garden and we spent all our time playing around it and, of course, climbing it. My father always told us not to climb the tree, but as soon as he was out of sight, we would all climb up and jump from the highest branch. My parents were more worried about us getting hurt than we were ourselves.

I remember that the tree (which is still there) had two very big branches which we called the Donkey and the Horse. The bigger one was the Horse and the smaller one, the Donkey. You could sit on them as though you were astride. We also had apple trees in the garden so there was always a good supply of apple tart in our house.

We lived on a farm, so needless to say, no farm is complete without chickens or hens. My job every morning was to go out to collect the eggs. My mother would warn me to be careful bringing in the eggs and not to run with them. As soon as I would have them gathered, I would run to the house and of course I would fall. Then the tears would fall because the eggs were broken. I think that, because I was the youngest girl, I was a 'pet' and my mother never gave out to me for breaking the eggs — every morning.

I have very fond memories of a very happy childhood, spending carefree, happy days playing with family and friends.

Music was a major influence in our house. Both my parents played and sang (my father played saxophone for many years with a local band). Sing-songs were part and parcel of our lives for family celebrations as they still are today. Everyone was required to entertain, be it a song, a tune or a poem, even a joke. I'm delighted to say that this tradition is still carried on within the family. Nowadays, my nieces and nephews all participate.

MIKE MURPHY

At twelve years of age and after five immensely unsuccessful years in Terenure College, apart from rugby and athletics that is, my father decided that, to further my academic sensibilities, I should be sent to Synge Street CBS.

I turned up on a damp Monday morning to Synge Street which is, of course, close to the centre of Dublin. I was appalled by the darkness of the classrooms, the concrete yard, the high walls, the noise, and the casual violence of some of the brothers (not that I wish to knock the Christian Brothers because far too much of that has been done already and in many cases they were wonderful men).

I was desperately homesick for the bright classrooms and the green fields of Terenure College where I could spend endless hours' looking out of the window at the pastoral countryside, day-dreaming. I decided I would not remove my Terenure College cap. During class, I was obliged to fold it and put it in my pocket, but during the break between classes, I wore it.

This did not go down too well. Very badly, in fact. I was attacked by almost all the other boys in my class who tried to take my cap from me. I managed to hold onto it, however. Then, some of the teachers intervened and told me I was not allowed to wear my Terenure cap in Synge Street.

I got through the first day all right and lasted four more

days. By Thursday evening, I was still in possession of my by now rather tattered cap, but I had created more enemies than most people do in a lifetime. That night, I informed my father that he was going to have to tie me up and physically bring me back to Synge Street — I promised I would study harder if I went back to Terenure College and that I would never complain about school again.

By Friday morning I knew I was in with a chance. I took my cap off at lunch-time and did not wear it. People began to be nice to me. But I had an instinct that I had got my way. Right enough, on arrival home that afternoon, my mother informed me that my father had decided to send me back to Terenure on the following Monday.

A sad and pathetic little victory, you will say. And rightly so. But a victory nonetheless!

DAVID NORRIS

When I was a child, I lived on the border of Ballsbridge and Sandymount, in the heart of the now-ridiculed Dublin 4 area. Sandymount had, and to some extent still has, the atmosphere of a village. On winter evenings, a small group of us would go down to the village on roller skates to buy sweets. But our roller skates were the real roller skates — a skeletal metal frame that adjusted to your shoe size, leather straps, toe-caps fitted with a key and, of course, ball-bearing-filled wheels that struck sparks off the pavements and streets.

Occasionally, the skate straps broke, but down in the village, help at hand. A splendidly caustic Cork woman, Miss Milligan, with grey hair drawn back in a severe gun-metal bun, presided over the Sandymount Stores, an archetypal village hardware shop. It had knotted pine floors that creaked, rolls of chicken wire and clusters of watering cans suspended from the ceiling. Miss Milligan also sold crepe paper (green and scarlet), exploding caps for toy pistols and, of course, emergency replacements of skate straps. The shop had its own distinctive aroma compounded of wood shavings, creosote and paraffin oil.

Miss Milligan and her shop are now both long gone, even though her lovely curved glass shop-front survives. Gone also are Batts, the chemists, on its corner site with swing doors like a western saloon, Leverett and Fryes, Findlaters and Roddy's sweet shop.

In the last-named, we bought sixpence worth of aniseed balls, special mixture and bulls-eyes, fizzy bags, lucky dips, sailor's chew and honeycap bars. Sweets were then still crammed into glass jars with bakelite caps. This was before anyone knew of the relationship between smoking, lung cancer and heart disease, so when we felt especially sophisticated, we would buy five Woodbine cigarettes in an off-lime-green paper packet and one match. Then back we skated up to Wilfield Park to our own little private cul de sac where we sat under the street lamp on the lip of the pavement, discussing the really important things of life — pet dogs, rabbits and mice and the daring images of the cinema, Western marshals and Chicago gangsters.

Our dream life was fed by those marvellous occasional Saturday afternoon visits to the cinema, mostly in to town to the Regal Rooms and the Capitol, now vanished, and the recently closed Carlton. This was if we could persuade some older sibling into accompanying us, as we were well brought up children only likely to be taken to main-stream cinemas like the Metropole in the company of adults, where the wholesome entertainments of costume drama would only occasionally be supplemented by a deliciously grisly second feature starring Fabian of the Yard and narrated by the sepulchrally-voiced Edgar Lustgarten. When we could escape, of course, we headed straight for the squirming, screaming terror of features like *The Curse of the Mummy's*

Tomb at the Carlton, for which guilty and illicit pleasure we paid for nights afterwards with unexplained nightmares.

Spring was the Spring Show. Then it seemed all the Irish countryside converged upon the capital, florid-faced farmers admiring appropriately gigantic cattle, delightedly noting adult embarrassment when a pendulously-equipped stallion slowly unsheathed and sprayed the ground like a quadruped fire engine, or emptied what seemed like a front garden full of steaming dung. With what alacrity we collected leaflets on farm machinery, free samples of this and that, and little badges advertising chemical companies.

Summer seemed one long, drawn-out sun-filled afternoon, with late evening visits by steam train or car to the Dun Laoghaire baths, then still known as the Kingstown baths. There were no water slides or wave machines then, but rows of strictly segregated changing rooms with briny-damp concrete floors opening onto the children's pool and also the adults' pool, with its dangerously alluring deep end. On the way home we sank chattering teeth into slabs of Cleeve's toffee.

Trips into town were also a great excitement. Elvery's, Hely's, Switzer's and Pim's, toy departments of all kinds where one could collect Dinky models of the latest Austin A40 saloon car or little kits easily assembled of balsa wood, Spitfires and Hurricanes with a lump of lead in the nose to ensure that our one-and-threepence worth did not shoot skywards on a solo trip to interstellar space.

At the end of the long, uniform Wilfield Road, which we considered socially, intellectually and probably morally inferior to our four detached *cul de sac* houses in the loop of Wilfield Park, there was a cricket field, Pembroke Wanderers, which became Monkstown Rugby Club for the winter months. On long summer evenings, we played Cowboys and Indians in the high Pampas grass and charged up the embankment to watch the mailboat train taking its passengers out to the *Cambria*, the *Hibernia* and the elderly *Princess Maud*. Invariably someone caught a smut in the eye.

Were they really, as it seems now, such innocent days? Or perhaps it was just that, at the age of eight, ten or even fourteen, the world was thrilling, mysterious and full of wonder, as I have no doubt it still is to people of eight, ten and fourteen and even, perhaps, to those of us lucky enough not to have entirely abandoned that world of childhood, although we pose as more sophisticated in the wicked wisdoms of our adult life.

FERGAL O'BRIEN

At last the waiting was over. The day had arrived when the results of the entrance exams for secondary school were announced. I couldn't believe my luck. After much anxiety, I found out that I was going to be in the top class in my new school. The excitement increased when I realised that I was to be joined by most of my friends.

When the dust settled, bets started to be waged about who would receive the best reward from their parents. Brendan was going to get £100, Seán a bicycle, and David a ghetto-blaster. Hearing all this had made my eyes water, so as soon as the final bell went, I ran all the way home.

I burst in the door, threw down my jacket and schoolbag and ran to my mother to tell her my good news. On reaching her, I explained the situation.

'Mam, Mam! I got top grades in my exams! So did Brendan and Seán! They're probably getting money and a bike! What am I getting?'

On hearing this, my mother called me over to her. As her purse rested beside her, this appealed to me greatly. With pound signs in my eyes, I listened. But the purse was not touched and instead, my mother held out her arms, hugged me and said, 'I'm proud of you.'

Following this embrace, I went to my bedroom and with tears in my eyes, I thought how unlucky I was.

It is only in recent years that I've learned my lesson from this tale. Nowadays, my success is judged on whether or not my mother again says, 'I'm proud of you.'

VINCENT O'BRIEN

When I was seven years old, my father took me to Mallow races. It was the opening day, and a great occasion for the neighbourhood. The principal race was the Mallow May Cup of £500, which was a big sum in those days.

We lived some fifteen miles away and I remember travelling to the races by pony and trap. The great jockey, Steve Donoghue, was to fly from England and land on the course. Since few people had seen an aeroplane, this was a most exciting event.

Everyone was looking towards the skies but in vain, as no plane arrived. Eventually the race-course manager appeared on the steps of one of the stands and read a telegram saying that, owing to inclement weather conditions, Steve was unable to travel. There was great disappointment among the huge crowd.

ARNOLD J. O'BYRNE

Ringsend is a working-class suburb of Dublin. It was there that I was born in 1939 and where I lived for all of my childhood days.

In the period when I was growing up, there

138

was no television, certainly not in Ringsend. So our pleasures were either self-made or once a week going to the films, or as we would say, to the pictures. The local cinema was the Regal where the admission prices were thruppence to the hard seats in the front row, now referred to as the front stalls, fourpence for the soft seats at the back (the back stalls) and eight pence upstairs. In those days, upstairs was simply that. No use referring to it as the circle, because to us, a circle was something you drew with a compass.

Naturally, we only paid thruppence. You only went to the soft seats when you got older and if you were taking a 'moth' (girl). Occasionally, if we did not have the money, we would gate-crash. The method was simple, but fraught with certain dangers — not only for the crashers but, indeed, for everyone in the hard seats.

There was only one attendant for all of the downstairs section. When he would be at the back, someone would open the emergency doors at the front, immediately adjacent to the screen, and in we would run. The attendant's job was to catch us, clip our ears and throw us out. However, if he failed to identify the gate-crashers, he had what to him was a logical way of meting out justice. He would estimate how many got in free and then he would choose a like number and eject them. Needless to say, those who got in free had great fun seeing the admission payers being thrown out. No arguments were allowed. If you were chosen, out you went.

Stretching from Ringsend seawards is the Pigeon House Road. This connects with the South Wall which runs out into Dublin Bay, ending at what is known as the Red Lighthouse. It was from this wall that we, as children, did most of our swimming. The distance from Ringsend church to the lighthouse would be about two and a half miles.

Getting to our swimming place was like traversing both an obstacle and an adventure course. The road stretched like a long finger out into the bay. On one side flowed the River Liffey, while on the other side lay Sandymount

Strand. Located on the strand side was St Catherine's, a tuberculosis hospital. As children, it was our belief that to take breaths as you passed the hospital could result in catching TB. Consequently, before we passed, we would fill our lungs with 'uncontaminated' air and run. Getting past the hospital, we would immediately open our mouths to expel the air and take in fresh air, only to be greeted by the most pungent, odious stench one could imagine. The stench came from the filter beds which lay immediately beyond the hospital but on the river side of the road. These filter beds took Dublin's sewage — and how we knew it. There was nothing for it but to fill our lungs with this foul-smelling air and gallop on, hoping soon to reach fresh air before collapse. I was never quite sure which was the better way to leave the world, effected by TB air or poisoned by sewage air.

The next stop was the Pigeon House fort. This had been vacated by the British in 1902, although much of its walls and the ramparts remained. This was an ideal place for boys with vivid imaginations and a sense of adventure in which to play and explore. On one occasion, we found an opening of some twenty feet deep with a trap door at the bottom. Motivated by curiosity and, with hindsight, a false sense of bravado, we returned to Ringsend hardware shop, pooled our money and bought a rope. Then we drew lots, with the winner being the lucky boy to be lowered down. I am sure on that day, heaven was bombarded with prayers from each of our group requesting not to be lucky! When the winner was chosen, the rest all gave suitable false expressions of bitter disappointment.

The rope was tied and down Our Hero went. Many words of advice, such as 'Watch out for rats and snakes', were thrown at Our Hero, whose feet barely touched the bottom when he was pleading to be raised again, claiming the trap door was locked, bolted and secured for life and that not even Superman could break it. As the group, at that moment, lacked a replacement Hero, no one was prepared to utter any words of disbelief.

Then it was on to our swimming place.

We had a choice of three, all situated at various points on the South Wall. These were the Costelloes, the White Rocks and the Half-Moon. At the latter, the men swam naked, so as well as being a good place to swim, there was a sense of acceptance in being able to swim naked as well.

It was rare in those days for women to walk out along the Wall, and if any did, they were seen in plenty of time to allow the men either to put on their togs or wrap a towel around themselves.

The warning signal of approaching females was a cry of 'Woman on the Wall'. Each word was drawn out, with the word 'Waaaall' receiving the greatest stretch. This would then be echoed in turn by each one present. Like something that had been rehearsed for decades, a solitary cry of 'Woman on the Waaaall' would go out, to be followed by another voice, then another and another and so on.

Never in unison.

And when the last man had had his turn, it was ours. Deepening our voices as much as possible and expanding our chests, we would then, in turn, take our turn, 'Woman on the Waaaall'.

On many a summer day, the gentle breeze would carry that cry out into the bay where I was convinced the residents in Howth heard it.

BRENDAN O'CARROLL

Brendan's Vertical Voyages

The recollections of any one person who spent their childhood in the Dublin of the 1960s would fill the National Library. To single out just one as being more memorable than the rest would be near on impossible.

For instance, I remember standing aghast in O'Connell Street surrounded by the rubble of Nelson's Pillar. I saw John F. Kennedy pass by the front of Clery's. I witnessed the last military parade go through the town on Easter Sunday, and I cheered loudly as I ran alongside the Buzz Aldrin, Michael Collins and Neil Armstrong cavalcade on their return from the moon. On one occasion, I even stood beside the man who threw the egg at Richard Nixon's car on his less than memorable visit to Dublin. The gardai piled into that section of the crowd, if I remember, and after a scuffle (in which I received a bloody nose), he was dragged away.

These were all great 'moments' in my childhood. However for this collection, I think I will reflect on one of the memories that provided me, if even for a short while, with a constant source of happiness. It began in April 1966. I was on one of my 'walk-abouts'. Let me explain. . . .

Me dad had passed away when I was young and me mammy was running a shelter for women. Each day, I finished school at 2.30 in the afternoon, but me mammy didn't get home until 5.30. So it was that I filled the time between 2.30 and 5.30 by wandering the city streets for the afternoon. Taking in the colour of the markets, the melodies of Moore Street and the Iveagh Market, I stood smiling as I watched the ladies stroll up and down Grafton Street, each one trying to walk posher than the other.

On this particular walk-about, I had confined myself to the north-west side of the Liffey. Down Liffey Street to Hector Grey's where I would tinker with the new marvels that had made their way here in the big boat from China. I was a big fan of Hector Grey's. My teacher, Mr Flood, had told us one day a little of Hector Grey's life story. How he would write 'tips' for the dog racing and sell them each night at the dog track for one shilling. By 1966, I reckoned Hector Grey was one of the richest men in the whole world. This proved, Mr Flood told us, that any man with an idea, the will to work and a hard neck could achieve anything his heart desired. I figured I was in with a chance.

I had lots of ideas and I couldn't wait to work.

However, as I walked around Hector's store in Liffey Street, feeling my neck, it still felt very soft. To this day when I walk down Liffey Street and pass by Hector's old shop, I touch the back of my neck and smile.

After Hector Grey's, I would head down to the Blarney Woollen Mills right at the Ha'penny Bridge and watch the strong man break out of his chains or tear a phone book in two. It's funny how different people think different ways; I am sure those around me in his audience were wondering how he did it. I just wondered where he got all the phone books.

From there I would head down to the CIE lost-and-found office on the quays. I paid a visit here maybe once a month. I would walk up to the counter and, when asked what I wanted, would say, 'Did anybody hand in a purse left on the No. 46 today?' Or maybe I'd say, 'Did anybody hand in a umbrella left on the No. 11 today?' The man would look through his journal, shake his head and apologise that there was no sign of the goods. I became such a regular that sometimes when I'd walk through the door, he'd just say, 'Hi, nothing for you today,' and smile.

I strolled down Litton Lane into Middle Abbey Street and glanced up at the *Irish Independent* clock; it was still only four o'clock. To this day I don't know why, but I began walking towards the entrance to the *Independent* offices which was just beneath the clock. I went in the entrance and stood in a dark hallway. There was a large door on my left with a frosted-glass panel and a large door facing me with a frosted panel, and beside that door protruding from the wall, there was what seemed to be some kind of cage.

Suddenly there was a hum from the cage, and what looked like a big steel plate at the back shot up and disappeared up a dark tunnel. I stepped back, a little scared, and was amazed to see a kind of steel basket inside the cage come shooting down the tunnel. It stopped about three feet from floor level.

I could see the bottom half of the body and the legs of a man. He had his left hand on a brass handle and he jerked it back and forth, and in little jumps, the basket sank slowly to ground level. He then pulled the brass handle back all the way, pulled back part of the cage, pulled back the outside of the cage and stepped out onto the floor. He said hello to me and walked straight out the front door into the street.

Believe it or not, I had never seen an elevator before. I glanced around to be sure that no one was looking and I stepped into the basket; it seemed to bounce as I stepped on it. The brass handle which the man had been pushing back and forward was set in a kind of half-moon slot. At one end of the slot it said 'Up'. At the other end it said 'Down'. And in the centre it said 'Stop'. I slid the handle back and forward a couple of times but nothing happened, so I returned it to the 'Stop' section.

Suddenly, way above me, I heard a voice cry, 'Close the bloody doors, for God's sake!'

I immediately leaned over and closed the door. Then I realised that the outside gate was still open, so I opened the inside gate, closed the outside and closed the inside gate. The elevator jerked into life and how I didn't crap in my pants I'll never know.

As it shot upwards, I nearly began to cry, thinking I was going to go through the roof. I saw the floors seeming to whiz by me and people actively walking around the cage, not even paying a ha'penny's worth of attention to me.

The elevator came to a bouncy halt at the fourth floor. A man was waiting there. He quickly opened both gates and stepped in, closed the gates again without paying any heed to me, took the brass handle and pushed it to 'Down'. The cage plummeted. As we neared the bottom, he pulled the handle back to stop. He left it about a foot short, so he moved it quickly forward and back again and it came to ground level. He opened the cage doors, exited and closed the cage doors after him.

For a few moments, I didn't move. I just stared at the

brass handle and in my mind I could hear it screaming at me — 'Push me, push me'. So I did.

I moved the handle to the 'Up' bracket and the elevator shot up. At the third floor, I pushed it to 'Stop' and the bloody thing did! However, the floor was at my waist level, so I eased the elevator up to be level with the floor. For the next quarter of an hour I went up and down, stopping at each floor unmolested and unhindered. It was easy to drive, this elevator.

Before long I could stop it bang on the floor first time, every time. Then a funny thing happened. I had brought the elevator down to ground level and was surprised to see a man standing outside the cage, waiting to come into the elevator. He opened both cage doors, closed them and instead of the expected scolding, said to me, 'Third floor, like a good man.' I pulled the handle to the 'Up' position. The elevator shot up and I stopped it bang on the third floor. He quickly exited. I took on two more passengers. One said, 'Fourth floor' and the other said 'Ground'.

I operated 'my' elevator Monday to Friday from 2.30 to 5 o'clock from then on. Every Friday, I would stay late until maybe 6.30 or 7, because on Friday I collected my tips. A thruppenny bit here, a couple of coppers there — even the odd sixpence. For some reason, I got the nickname in there of 'Benny', a name still used by my closest friends today.

For the first time in my life, I felt I was going places, even if it was just up and down. The people who worked in the *Independent* and the *Herald* smiled at me as they entered the elevator and would rub my hair fondly. For the first time, I felt like I belonged to the human race and was not just a spectator. Even today, the smell of printing ink lifts my heart and I can understand why those in the newspaper industry can be passionate about their business. I remembered it as a wonderful, pulsating world where something was happening all the time. So if there are still any of those old codgers left from the Indo or the Herald of '66, please accept a heartfelt 'Thanks' from Benny, the lift boy, who for one spring in '66, felt he just might be another Hector Grey.

Regrettably, this only lasted three months, until July of 1966, for my mother put me on a plane and packed me off to my sister in Walthamstow, London E17. It was there I was introduced to football and 'World Cup Willie' — but that's another story.

KEVIN O'CONNOR

Sister Perpetua's Apples

At that time, boys and girls were taught in different parts of the convent school. The only thing taller than Sister Perpetua was the wall that surrounded the orchard. Every day, after the raucous lunch break, two boys collected a bucketful of mush for the pigs which were fattened in a snorting pen at the back of the orchard.

The mush was the leavings of the bread and milk we were given in the break. The part-eaten slices of white bread, soggy with milk and snot, were collected, kneaded into lumps and put in the buckets. Every day, a different two boys carried the buckets through the orchard.

Mickser was my friend and the pal I most admired. Why wouldn't I? Hadn't he saved me from a beating the day I came in wearing a coat with a velvet collar?

'Yah, yah, little sissy!' came the shout of Runnynose, known for the way his snot dripped onto his bread.

I was being rolled around the yard, crying, when Mickser came to my rescue, fighting off Runnynose and Crop Head, who had the marks of ring-worm on his shaved skull. But they were no match for Mickser's hard knuckles. So when it came to our turn to bring up the mush and Mickser said, 'We'll get apples as well,' I was all for it.

'You hop in and get them — I'll stand watch,' he said. 'Then we'll bring them back in the empty buckets. Nobody will know.'

With the belief of a five-year-old in the assurance of a six-year-old who had fought off the two guys of seven, I hopped along the row, plucked the apples — and was met by Sister Perpetua as I came out through the avenue of trees, my arms loaded.

There was no sign of Mickser. He told me afterwards that he 'had to run back' when Sister Perpetua gave him a slap on the face with her hand, which must have been harder than the fists of Runnynose. She had bony fingers which held my arms tight all the way back to the yard. So Mickser was right to run, wasn't he?

My punishment was to be put 'in the girls' class' for a week. I cried even more there, and was let out after three days. I tried to be friends with Mickser again, but he didn't ask me to rob any more apples. I noticed he went around with Runnynose and Crop Head.

Between them, they would bash up other boys, especially fellas with nice clothes. But they left me alone 'cos I had been in the girls' school — a place where no one, not even fellas they called 'Sissy', had ever been before and come back alive.

SINÉAD O'CONNOR

I Remember my Granny

My mother's mother. Kitty was her name. And she lived on Keeper Road in Crumlin. She came originally from Waterford, though. Her name was Roach before she got married, and then it became O'Grady. Like in 'O'Grady says'. That game is all about my granny, y'know!

I liked her 'cos she smoked. And I liked the smell. And she had a cackley-croaky laugh because of it. And she had nice teeth.

Her hair was black. And then it was orange, and then it was whitey. With nicotine stains at her forehead. She had brown fingers from smoking too. I loved watching her smoking a fag.

When all the others and my mother had gone out, my granny made me strong, sweet tea. And tomato sandwiches with loads of salt, which I was not normally allowed have, and it was a great secret between us.

After she had made the tea, she would sit at the end of the table and light up her fag and let me blow out the match.

'There's an angel that came to visit us,' she'd say. 'Do you want to blow it out?'

I'd let it burn right up to her fingers before I'd want the angel to leave. I loved fire. I liked sticking my stilts in the fire when I was a child, to get the ends burning so that I could walk across the floor with feet of fire. DO NOT TRY THIS! It only leaves smelly, melted rubber on the carpets which will not come off and is bound to get you into serious trouble!

My granny, I should let you know, was also my godmother. And she therefore still is, even though her body is not here any longer. She looks after me, and does the job.

I remember how she would smoke in silence. Standing at the end of the table. I watched her from the couch, facing her under the window. Her arms folded, or playing with her hair. She would smoke silently and cry. All silently.

What I loved most about my granny was her silence. *Our* silence. We had a very silent relationship. We did not speak much when we were alone together. We did not need to. In our silence, we communicated with each other. Just by being with each other. We felt each other and didn't need to speak 'human-talk'. The silence was calm, and not eerie.

She was a fairy, my granny, and I know she was because she used to hypnotise me with her eyes. She was my mother, really. Her face close to mine.

She'd just look really, really into my eyes, and her eyes were almost navy-blue and black. And it seems to me that the coloured part swirled, and I fell asleep. I love the moon and the stars and the blue that is at night, because they remind me of her eyes.

She calls me her little chicken when she tucks me into bed. And she puts her finger to her lips and says 'Shh, now. Hush, hush.'

GAY O'DRISCOLL

My earliest memory of football is of summertime in Ownachincha in West Cork where we lived at the time. Ownachincha was then a place where the local people from the surrounding hinterland would come on Sundays and spend the afternoon at the beach. Every Sunday, the sound of Michael O'Hehir's voice could be heard on transistor radios on the roof of a car or on the Warren, with groups of people huddled around listening to the progress of the championship.

I can remember one Christmas when Santa brought me a leather football. Each Sunday throughout all that summer, I would play football on a flat part of the Warren across the road from our house with whomever came along while a neighbour would do a perfect take-off of Michael O'Hehir. My mother recalls many times how I would sit on the bank with my real football and when enough lads would come along, two teams would be made up and away we would go. According to my mother, all of these lads were older and bigger than me and I would run up and down and never get a kick of the ball. But to me, I was contributing greatly to the match. When the match finished or some of the lads got tired and continued on their way or whatever, I would go back to sitting on the bank and wait for the next group to be formed and have another match. This would go on until it got too dark and bed was an attractive proposition for a tired seven-year-old.

We moved to Dublin in 1957 and I went to school in Marino and I remember a football book was for sale in the office. I went to buy it and Brother O'Neill, who was in charge of games in the school at that time, asked me if I was interested in football and whether I had played in West Cork. I then proudly informed him I had not only played for the Rosscarberry under-14 school team but we won the school shield that year and I scored a goal. I did not tell him, however, how I scored the goal, which was again not unlike me running up and down across from my house and not getting a kick of the ball. A high ball came in and hit the cross-bar with me running in after it. The ball rebounded, hit me straight in the face and went into the goal and we won. We then came back to Rosscarberry and had a great celebration and the head master drove me home quite late to my concerned mother as she awaited the result.

Having told my little story, Brother O'Neill asked me to turn up for training for the school team and to go to St Joseph's in Fairview at 7.00 pm the following Thursday and sign up for the local club.

I then went home and gave all the arrangements to my mother and father. The book turned out to be a book on St Vincent's. The local club was also St Vincent's and the rest, as they say, is history.

BILL O'HERLIHY

The Day Ring became Clark Kent

It is a day burned into my memory, but don't ask me to quote chapter and verse in detail. Cork were playing Limerick in the Munster championship and I was on holiday on Sherkin Island off Baltimore, West Cork.

These were the days before television and the conversation on John Willie's boat on the morning of the match was based on the word-pictures of Mick O'Hehir's radio commentaries and the very special skills of a man called Ring.

It's hard today to imagine that scene on Sherkin: more than twenty of us, fathers, sons and probably first cousins once removed, crowded around the kitchen radio, soaking up the images offered by O'Hehir.

As the game progressed, the mood darkened and, if we were correctly reading O'Hehir, Cork were gone. But how could we have reckoned without Ring? Out of the blue, a goal, and we were encouraged; another and we were cheering. Astoundingly, a third in five minutes and we were ahead — and you would not believe the shouting and cheering and dancing in that kitchen.

To those of us in that kitchen, Ring was Clark Kent translated in five minutes to immortality as Superman. Cork won that day because of Ring's genius. It wasn't something entirely new, Ring's genius, but it was rarely so sensationally defined. He was to all of us in Cork, men and boys, the greatest hurler who ever lived, and we walked from the kitchen that day with the very special glow of certainty.

There is, I reckon, a swagger which comes naturally to all Cork folk who take their sport seriously. Ring on the big match days he revelled in, and the likes of the Kiernans, Tom and Michael, Noel Cantwell, Noel Murphy, Jimmy Barry, Billy Coleman and Billy Morgan and latterly Roy

Keane and Denis Irwin have brightened our spirits on many a gloomy day.

But even among those great sportsmen, Ring was the greatest and so acknowledged by all. When he wore the red jersey of Cork, he had a special bonding influence which overcame the petty parochialism of Cork hurling of the time. That was what that day on Sherkin was all about — Christy Ring, weaver of my boyhood dreams, my childhood hero who lives forever.

PADRAIG O hUIGINN

When a young boy in Cork city during the thirties, I learned a lesson in diplomacy which has stood me in good stead ever since.

An American battleship put into Cork harbour and there were a lot of crewmen who had Cork connections. My mother had an uncle who worked in the Harbour Commissioners and he was envious of all the people who were coming to collect relatives from the ship. A colleague, noting this envy, decided to play upon it. He told the uncle that he had been on the ship and met a man called Daly who might, therefore, be a relative.

The uncle, only too ready to believe that he might meet a long-lost cousin, sent an invitation, via the colleague, to Mr Daly to come and visit the family. We were all gathered in the uncle's house on the fateful evening to meet our Daly cousin, the tables laden with food and drink. There was much speculation about to which related family in the States he belonged.

Finally, the door opened and in walked a tall, handsome man — who was black! This was a big surprise in Cork in the thirties, where a black person was rare. I had never seen one except in films.

My uncle realised he was duped, but rose to the occasion magnificently. 'What is your name, son?' he said.

'Michael Daly, sir' the sailor replied.

The uncle immediately said, 'There never was a Michael in our family, but you are very welcome, son.'

There followed a good party to which the sailor contributed many tales of sailing on the rough seas in his battleship.

By the end of the evening, we were convinced he was a cousin!

OLIVIA O'LEARY

All winter long, it sat on the upstairs landing. It had wooden slats, and leather and metal fastenings. We scraped our legs as we played chase around it on rainy days. It had taken our mother half-way around the world, but we didn't rate things that happened before we were born. And this was just an old thing.

Until May. Until that moment when my mother opened the lid and released the smell of mothballs and cotton. Until summer escaped from the trunk.

Then our landing turned into a stage. We fought over faded clothes abandoned last September. There was the smart American beach-dress we coveted every year but never wore because summers on the Barrow never got that smart — or that warm. There was the slithery 1930 tennis dress that we shrieked over, but sort of fancied. Some of us had grown over the winter into a whole harvest of summer dresses. Some of us weren't so lucky. The comfortable shorts from last year were tight to bursting point. The blouse wouldn't fasten. My mother would hint diplomatically at a dress-making session.

'We'll get a Vogue pattern,' she'd say decisively. When in doubt, my mother always bought a Vogue pattern.

By the end of the afternoon, there were clothes everywhere — sliding down the banisters, hanging off the door-knobs. Smaller girls were floating around in wrinkled old party dresses. I was persuading myself into the 1930s tennis dress. My uncle's fencing gear, stowed at the very bottom of the trunk, was getting an airing somewhere outside.

My dad would arrive home in the middle of all this and grab his own piece of finery — a child's sun-hat, more than likely, with embroidered flowers. He'd fool around in it for a while and then forget about it. Late into the evening, it would still be parked on his head, forgotten. We'd stare and him and explode into giggles when he asked us why.

He never got annoyed. He put it down to something silly and happy. Something which had escaped, like summer, from the trunk.

ANDY O'MAHONY

School-days in Clonmel during the war. That's the Second World War, for those of you who care about fine distinctions of this kind. There was a rumour that the Germans had landed at Dungarvan. Later, our elders were known to have believed that the chosen landing site played a crucial role in the grand geo-military scheme of things. It was as if Hitler and his advisers had spent days agonising over whether it should be Dungarvan or Tramore.

Even as school-children, we were very proud at the thought of the German military machine having its ultimate eye on Clonmel. Not that we were overawed by this. After all, we lived in a town that had survived the unwanted attentions of Oliver Cromwell. The west gate at one end of Irishtown was a constant reminder of that. On this occasion, however, it was the other end of Irishtown that was the focus of attention, that part of it which adjoins the Convent Bridge. We knew that if a single German tank made its appearance at the top of Irishtown, then the mines on the bridge had not done their job.

No tanks did appear. The invasion of Dungarvan was no more than a rumour. But the memory of that day remains. The heady mixture of fear and excitement endures. Our elders everywhere in animated colloquy. The look-out spot from the windows of a red-brick house at the top of Irishtown facing the Convent Bridge. Grey skies. The waiting.

MICHEAL Ó MUIRCHEARTAIGH

Con Reardon, the Travelling Man

I have a great liking for card-playing which can be traced back to my childhood in Kerry.

Then as now, the travelling people traversed the roads of Ireland, and Kerry was on the itinerary of some such folk. I have a clear recollection of the names of several of them because they were more than anonymous callers when they visited the homes of the area. There were Mikey and Tommy Coffey, Blind Noney, the beautiful Roseanne Maloney, and the prince among all road men, Con Reardon.

I learned my love of card-playing from the same Con. He was a man of great elegance and he always travelled alone. His companions could be named as a pack of cards and some light merchandise which he sold to customers who always seemed anxious to buy. He dealt mostly in shoe laces and the stronger variety known locally as 'fongs', laces made from leather.

But it was his card-playing which fascinated me, as it was his custom to sit by the side of the road whenever tiredness overtook him. The cards would be produced and while the world passed by, anyone who had a moment to dally would be welcome to sit and take a hand of cards from the bearded knight of the roads.

He taught the subtleties of dealing, leading, holding and reading cards as only a professor could and I was frequently a willing pupil when on my way home from school.

He was never short of a roof over his head when night came and I can recall him spending a few 'stays' in our home. The pack would again be produced on such occasions and I used to marvel at his dexterity of hand as he spun the cards on the table.

But his talents were not confined to card-playing alone by any means. While nobody knew nor worried about his background, it seemed that he was a well-educated person who had a great command of the English language. He was a good storyteller and there was magic in the way he would sometimes preface a tale by saying 'When I was in India' or some other such faraway place.

We didn't question — it was the age of trust.

He was also a brilliant reader, as was discovered by chance. At the time it was not unknown for the person nearest the lamp to be given the chore of reading the paper aloud for the benefit of those assembled in the rambling house. On one particular night, Con was present and the standard of the reading must not have been to his liking, because he interrupted with a remark that lived on for a generation: 'Fetch me that paper until I throw some light on it.'

His request was granted and we were treated to a performance which even Richard Burton in his heyday could be proud of. Needless to say his powers were used again and again.

No wonder we looked forward to his visits and his kindly words of 'God save all here' as he crossed the threshold.

BRENDAN O'REILLY

I come from the town of Granard, Co. Longford, much of which was burned down during the Black and Tan War. And this probably explains why I heard such a lot about that troubled period when I was growing up there in the thirties.

Granard was also the home town of Kitty Kiernan, the fiancée of the man who is now referred to as Ireland's greatest revolutionary, Michael Collins. The Kiernan family lived across the street from the O'Reillys and nearby was the home of my godmother, Eily Flood, where Collins stayed on occasion when he was visiting Kitty. I too used hear my father and Eily, who had been a member of *Cumann na mBan*, talking with great affection about Collins and some of their stories conjure up images of the time.

One winter's evening, Collins and Sean McKeown were expected to visit the Floods. Eily Flood, who played piano and my father, James P., who sang and played the violin, decided to have a musical evening at Floods to act as a decoy for the arrival of the two wanted men.

James P. was singing a song called 'The Deathless Army' when the parlour door opened and in came Collins, followed by McKeown, in full volunteer's uniform. The music stopped and everyone stood up. When greetings were exchanged, Collins asked the company to take their seats again and let James P. finish the song, which he did.

After the applause, Collins put his hand on the head of my eldest brother Frank, who was nine years of age at that time, and said, 'I hope you grow up to be as good a singer as your father.' Frank, who is now in his eighties and living in northern California, remembers it well. James P., who in later years was proud of having been invited by Count John McCormack to sing a duet with him at a concert in Granard, was equally proud of having been asked by Collins to finish the song.

On another occasion, Collins and Harry Boland were asleep in a bedroom at the top of the Flood house when Black and Tans, on a house-to-house inspection, banged on the street door. Eily saw them through a curtain from a first floor window and dashed upstairs to the bedroom where the two were sleeping. Having raised the alarm, she then came slowly down the stairs to the front door. She opened it and stepped outside, deliberately closing it behind her but pretending that it was an accident. It was a very brave thing for her to do, as people had been shot by the Tans for a lot less. They swore at her and threatened to kill her, ordering her to go up the lane by the side of the house and open the door.

'I felt the bullet in my back all the way up the lane,' she said. She kept calm, however, and gave Collins and Boland time to escape out the back of the house and away.

She told other stories of bringing messages to Dublin for Collins, and of Collins dousing Harry Boland with water to wake him up. It was the kind of chat I used to hear, sitting by the fireside in Granard in the days before radio and television.

TONY O'REILLY

The Time of Our Lives

No, not your snotty maths teacher explaining some Pythagorean logic on a dull afternoon, but the sonorous voice of Father Dinan of Blackrock College, humbly asserting that, yet again, Blackrock had won the Leinster schools' cup. To those who have experienced it, the exquisite pain can be felt across the years. A blizzard of blue and white scarves, a proud mother (not yours — theirs), a cup held aloft and on its way home to its rightful place in the Castle.

As Bob O'Connell, the surgeon and wit, used to say: 'Ye always know Blackrock boys, they rattle.'

'With what?' I said.

'With medals,' he replied. 'Big boys, small boys, thin boys, fat boys, they all have medals. You'd be a leper out there,' he said, 'if ye weren't on a cup winning team.'

Happily, a more egalitarian tone exists today and schools unheard of in my time — Tempelogue, CBC Monkstown and St Michael's — hold eminent sway in the contest each year. My God, even Clongowes, where Jesuit fathers rusticate before taking on the full rigours of Belvedere, ＾i＇ cups with some regularity nowadays.

And so it is upon us again, the season of the I＿＿＿r schools' cup. Having played in thirty-nine inter＿＿＿＿l rugby matches, I can state quite categorically tha＿＿＿＿ is nothing like schools' rugby anywhere in the w＿＿ The whole year hangs on it — and even more so in ＿＿ni＿ cup. It's the first time you will know what nerve＿ are all about.

Mothers become obsessively devout. Fathers disappear mysteriously from important meetings. Prayer assumes a new meaning. God is reduced to a figure with whom you negotiate directly. And as each round passes, you become the fulcrum of the school's attention, your every move and injury talked about, your prowess all that stands between the school and two full free days if you win the cup. The converse, of course, is too painful to mention — no places in the history books and Shakespeare's 'Mere Oblivion'.

But take heart, even if you don't succeed, you will make friends that will last you a lifetime. I've even come to like O'Leary, Brophy, Cleary, McDonnell, Cox, Greham, Woods, Turley, Keegan, Tubridy, Pembrey, O'Sullivan, Kenny and McCarthy. I've even come to love a man who became one of my closest friends and who epitomised the spirit of rugby football, the late 'Locky' Butler. Even my memory of the humble Father Dinan and his apostle, Father Hampson, has warmed with the passage of time. But my mother never forgave them!

PEADAR O RIADA

Ag Fiach

A large chunk of my childhood memories are of sun-dappled days, running underneath trees, by streams or over stone walls and ditches. Some of these times were spent in the pursuit of rabbits with so-called 'hunting dogs'. A hunting hound was basically a mongrel dog of sheepdog extraction but with a prized trace of greyhound blood in some remote part of its lineage.

We roamed in groups of three, four or five and, as it was the age of innocence, our travels had covered many miles by evening's close. We never actually caught a rabbit and so did not have to come to that awful decision on the life or death of another creature. Oddly enough, we could get quite jealous of those among us who were lucky enough to find a baby rabbit. Raising one of these wild animals was a challenge in itself and much discussion would take place at school as how best to get it to survive on a diet of watered and sugared cow's milk. These conferences usually took place at the 'play-hour' as the unfortunate baby rabbit was passed from one to another before being replaced inside the lucky owner's shirt or gansey, there to rest, warm, until classes were over.

At night, my father used to read stories of Fionn Mac Cumhaill and the Fíanna to us. Their fantastic feats of glory and valour became part of our waking and sleeping dreams.

When I was about twelve, all of these factors came together in one incident. My father gave me a present of an actual, real hound. It was a three-month-old, great, big, lolloping Irish wolfhound. My father had received him from his own good friend, Garech de Brún. I called the hound Fionn and his arrival meant that dreams of the Fíanna and their famous hounds, Sceolán and Bran, were now more tangible.

However, the dog also howled all night, every night! Then there was all the big, big mess to be cleaned up every morning — the dog slept by the fire in the kitchen, d'you see?

But worst of all, this noble hound had no interest whatsoever in hunting. He dawdled and whimpered along, far behind the rest of us and the other more vigorous dogs. This meant that we had to stop running and wait for him every five or ten minutes. He most definitely was no steeple-chaser and even the most unobtrusive ditch meant a major lifting session to get him to the other side. He was heavy.

But he was mine and one of the first loves of my life. He was a most noble and loyal creature and lived many years, a constant companion as I grew into manhood, through both good and bad times.

I hope my children will be as lucky and can enumerate such happy memories of childhood among their daydreams in later life.

COLM O'ROURKE

If the real wealth of a childhood can be measured by the store of happy memories, then I certainly have riches beyond compare. Life was all about enjoyment and even school, which is the bane of many young people's existence, does not appear to have been treated with the sort of seriousness it now enjoys. Certainly, the dreaded homework took little or no time compared with the amount of effort my own children put into it each night.

The early years were spent growing up in Aughavas in south Leitrim. My father was a farmer, which meant that a family of twelve, eight boys and four girls, was going to enjoy little in the way of monetary benefits in the fifties and sixties. Rossan national school was the first port of call in the educational world, and I can recall the anxious waiting for the opening of the school football pitch, which was closed up for the winter, as heralding the arrival of summer. I now realise that this ground, which in my mind was the closest thing imaginable to Croke Park, was so short that any decent juvenile would kick a ball the full length of the pitch. I can also remember my brother Padraig coming to collect me from school and bringing me home on the back of his bike while performing plenty of acrobatic manoeuvres for my benefit on the way.

Football played a big part in my childhood; with seven older brothers who were all keen participants, it is hardly surprising. After we moved to Meath in 1966 when I was nine years old, I dreamt of playing some day in Croke Park for the Royal County and luckily, that part of my dreams has worked out fairly well.

My first chance to watch a big game in Croke Park was the 1967 All-Ireland final between Meath and Cork. Then, my brother Padraig carried me in on his shoulders and I watched the match sitting on his knee in the Cusack Stand. There were no big worries at that time about lifting children over the turnstiles or about safety regulations, and most kids' love of Gaelic games was nurtured through being carried in to big matches like I was, nearly thirty years ago.

Home life was always contented. There was always plenty of fun going on with such a big family, and our house became an attraction for all the neighbours, as there was always a guarantee of quickly getting a match going which was participated in by both boys and girls, long before ladies' football started.

Life was fairly simple for me back then, as on every farm there was plenty of work to be done. Daddy ensured we all had our jobs, but the introduction of a ball could cause immediate suspension of duties. While money always seemed scarce, I wanted for nothing. Food always seemed plentiful and Mammy not only fed her own crew but also anyone else who stopped by. Whether it was the wandering tramps of the day or the best-off person in the parish, it made no difference to her.

Christmas was a great occasion in our house. With everyone home, there could have been eighteen or twenty for dinner on occasions. Presents were small, as Santa did not bring bikes, computer games or Manchester United outfits then. It was a simpler and, in many ways, a better society. It is not hard to make a child happy, once you are well cared for with love and affection. Everything else is secondary and I would wish for every child growing up in this country to be as happy as I was in my childhood.

MARY O'ROURKE

We all have lovely memories of the past. Somehow when we were young, the sun always shone in the summer, the ice creams seemed bigger, the friends seemed more loyal and the world stretched ahead of us, an endless vista of enjoyment and fun. One could call it *la vie en rose*. But even in all those happy memories, certain incidents often stand out which never leave your mind, and which from time to time are worth repeating and recalling.

There were four children in our family — Brian, Paddy,

Ann and myself. Brian, Paddy and Ann were seven, six and five years older than me respectively. And like all younger and last children, I always seemed to be striving to keep up with the other three. Being 'all of an age' together, so to speak, they formed their own gang and never wanted to have me tagging along. I was too much of a baby in their eyes and always wanting to go home when the slightest mishap befell any of us. So I had to develop strategies (but that was a grand word which I would not have understood then) to deal with all of this. And in the way of the young, I soon did.

We were a political family and in the forties, I recall many eminent figures coming to our house where we lived at General Textiles in Athlone. One particular occasion stands out in my mind — I think it must have been the general election of 1948 — when Éamon de Valera came to Athlone to address a huge rally in the Market Square. This was a time when these rallies attracted large numbers, with every partisan in robust voice and indeed often ending in minor fisticuffs.

In 1948 I was eleven years of age, and was allowed with my three siblings to go to hear de Valera. He came to visit our house afterwards and Brian, Paddy and Ann were allowed to join with all the Party faithful in animated discussion and chat in the 'big room' as we called it, a sort of extended kitchen/living room/sitting room. I was packed off to bed amid howls of anger and no cajolery would pacify me.

However, I was pushed firmly into bed. Up the corridor I could hear the loud talk, the laughter, the argument growing more intense as time went on. Nothing would do me but to be part of it. So I crept out of bed and up the corridor. I got myself a cushion and plonked myself outside the door, listening, listening, listening. If I close my eyes now, I can still see myself, the dark corridor, the soft cushion, the closed door, the gaiety, the warmth, the excitement which seemed to be beyond that door and I not a part of it. Oh, how I longed to be in the middle of that mysterious grown-up world of politics!

Forty-five years on, that memory is still strong and vibrant. For me, it was the start of a long love affair with politics and I'm still enraptured, enthusiastic and enthralled.

MICHAEL OSBORNE

A Tale from Punchestown Past

The clip-clop of hooves on the untarred road heralded the imminent arrival of another runner at Punchestown on Conyngham Cup day. The small, wizened groom with pigeon-toed gait could scarcely keep abreast of his charge.

'What's his name, Mister?' the young boy asked.

'Hold him there for a minute while I have a swig, and I'll tell you.'

Pulling a funny-shaped bottle from his inside pocket and a furtive glance up and down the road, he took a swig from the bottle and said, 'I've walked all the way from the Sallins train, and yesterday I walked all the way from my home to Limerick Junction, twenty-eight miles, and slept with this fellow in the same carriage all the way to Sallins. But it was worth it, because he will win the La Touche today.'

'But what's his name?' the young boy asked.

'Signal Hill, owned by a man in Tipperary. I'll bring you some liquorice sticks on the way back from the race.'

At five o'clock the groom returned, the saddle carried by his side, the bridle and tack sack slung over his shoulder, but no horse.

'Where's Signal Hill?' the young boy asked.

'He fell at the Big Double; he won't be going home. A horse of Mr J. V. Rank's called Slacker, ridden by P. P. Hogan and trained by Tom Dreaper, won it carrying fourteen stone.'

'Did you bring the liquorice sticks?'

'Oh! God, I forgot. I better be going — it's a long way to Tipperary.'

He emptied the bottle with one, long swig, shouldered his unwanted load of horse tack and, with a shortened step, disappeared slowly on the road to Naas.

All that afternoon, the boy's thoughts had been of the pride and joy of telling his classmates in the Green School next day, 'I held the winner of the La Touche at Punchestown yesterday.'

A shattered dream.

JACK O'SHEA

I have lots of happy memories from my childhood. I was one of a family of seven, one brother and five sisters, born in Cahirciveen, Co. Kerry. Our home was situated in the town itself, opposite the local GAA football pitch, which gave me so many of those happy memories. As a young boy, I spent most of my spare time in our local 'Croke Park', playing mini football games of Kerry versus Offaly, Kerry versus Down. It was always Kerry. I was always Mick O'Connell in my mind. My hero.

At about the age of nine, I can remember Mick O'Connell and Mick O'Dwyer coming together once or twice a week to practise and train together, wearing that famous green and gold. Watching both of them practise, 'the grace of Mick O'Connell', the determination and skills of Mick O'Dwyer. Oh, what a thrill this was for me! It was to get even better. They asked me if I would retrieve the balls for them when they went over the fence at the back of the goal-posts. Surely any boy's dream.

Around that time, our local boys' primary school was going on a school tour to Dublin. We were to visit Dublin Zoo, the museum — and Croke Park. I had never been outside of Co. Kerry before and I was really excited about visiting Croke Park. On our arrival there, I remember climbing the steps of the Hogan Stand, where the winning captains receive the Sam Maguire Cup. Looking out across the magic green turf and saying to myself, 'I would love to play here some day in an All-Ireland final.'

My next visit to Croke Park was to be nine years later. I was playing with the Kerry minor team in the All-Ireland semi-final. The place had not changed from the visit I had on that school tour. My dreams and ambitions as a footballer had come true. I had played on that famous turf which my two idols had graced before me.

JAMES PLUNKETT

The Blue, Remembered Hills

My paternal grandmother, a little woman who surprised me now and then by her free and easy use of strong language, confessed to me once that she believed in fairies. I was a sceptical child and it came to me as a great shock. Ghosts were all right; practically everybody knew someone who knew someone else who had seen one. The Banshee I accepted (I believed I had heard her keening one night myself). But fairies were beyond the sensible limit. I asked her what in God's name led her into such a strange notion. She told me she had seen them.

'Where?' I asked.

'In Glencullen,' she said. 'When I was a young girl and I in the fields milking the cows of a summer's morning, I'd see them riding down the mountain on their horses.'

'What horses?' I asked.

'White horses mostly,' she said, 'though there was the odd brown one.'

'And what were they like?' I asked, determined not to let her away with it.

'Little men,' she said, 'with green tunics and scarlet breeches. Do you not believe in fairies yourself?'

'I do not,' I said.

'Ah, well,' she said, taking the poker to stir the fire, a thing she always did when people downfaced her. 'Maybe there's none any longer. There's many a wonder gone out of the world since I myself was a child.'

Nevertheless, the next time I was in Glencullen I kept a sharp eye out, in case there might be a bit of excitement I might miss. I followed a little mountain stream for a long way up the hillside. The water was golden brown from bog and sunlight, it had whorls and rapids where thick clouts of foam spun round and round. The air smelled of gorse and thorn bushes, a warm, hungry smell. It looked like a good place for any band of fairies that knew their business, but there were none. The odd rabbit popped off with a flash of white scut, an old goat with a beard chased me through a clump of nettles which raised blisters on my bare legs. When I escaped, I rubbed them with dock leaves to stop the stinging. My grandmother, I decided, must have been a particularly gullible child. There was tea when I got back, with boiled eggs, home-made bread and jam and farmhouse butter. That is the first memory of many that still remain with me of the Dublin–Wicklow Mountains.

They are very beautiful, those mountains, much more to me than mere landscape. In childhood days, one travelled by pony and trap or by horse and cart, a slow, swaying way of doing it, with the roadside trees and hedges and stone walls meandering past the windows and the faint smell of leather upholstery in your nose and the crunching sound of the wheels in your ears and the jingle of harness. The shorter journeys were through Whitechurch and Pine Forest to Glencullen where there was always a stop at Fox's pub, strong refreshment for the men, lemonade and biscuits for me; or by Dundrum and the Scalp to Enniskerry, with the same trimmings at journey's end.

But the real adventure, which took up most of the day, was to travel over Sallygap to Glendalough by the military road. It led at the beginning past the Yellow House at Rathfarnham, where the soldiery had stopped for refreshment when escorting Robert Emmet's faithful young housekeeper, Anne Devlin, and her parents and relatives to prison. Then it carried on to Ballyboden and began to climb over the Featherbed Mountain. The Hellfire Club could be inspected on the way by climbing a steep mountain slope which revealed, as you went on your way, fine views of Pine Forest and Tibradden Mountain on the left and Dublin Bay and the coastline to the east.

The building itself had a look of ancient villainies about it. In the eighteenth century, the club was a wild rendezvous for the bucks and blades of the aristocracy. A place for drinking and gambling and for the rape of abducted heiresses, who felt they had to redeem their virtue by consenting to marriage with the young rake responsible. The bucks found it a quick way to restore an ill-spent inheritance. They used to celebrate Black Masses here too, or so local gossip had it. Then one day during a game of cards, someone looked under the table at the legs of the stranger who had joined the company and found he had a cloven hoof. It was the Devil himself. This appearance seems to have given the place a bad name. Anyway, it was allowed to fall into ruins. The story tempted some friends and myself to sleep in the ruins one Hallowe'en many years ago, when we were all about fourteen or fifteen years of age. The wind howled in the chimneys, the ruins creaked and groaned, everything seemed propitious, but the Devil failed to turn up. He had grown used to more aristocratic company.

Then on to Glencree where the huge barracks, long abandoned by the military, lit the imagination and filled the heart with excitement. It had been one of the strongholds built after the Rising of 1798 to keep in check the remnants of the Wicklow rebels still holding out in the hills. One of its commanders had been Sir John Moore who had parleyed there with the Wicklow leader, Michael Dwyer, giving him safe conduct for the purpose. One of the poems in *Palgrave's Golden Treasury* which we had to learn in school was about John Moore. It lamented his death in an engagement with the Spanish in 1809, when he was fatally wounded. In childhood, I would always remember the poem when we stopped at the barracks and still do whenever I visit it all these years later. It was called 'The Burial of Sir John Moore at Corunna' and the first two verses go:

> 'Not a drum was heard, not a funeral note,
> As his corpse to the rampart we hurried
> Not a soldier discharged his farewell shot
> O'er the grave where our hero we buried.
>
> We buried him darkly at dead of night
> The sods with our bayonets turning
> By the struggling moonbeams' misty light
> And the lantern dimly burning.'

That is only one of a host of memories which enrich any journey to the hills of Dublin and Wicklow.

MAUREEN POTTER

An unusual memory of my school-days is of Dinah, our pet rat. Dinah lived in a little hutch in our garden and one morning when I went to feed her, I found her dead. Then and there I decided to bring her to school as a present for the teacher — well, more of a surprise than a present.

This particular teacher took great exception to my getting time off from school to perform in afternoon shows at the Theatre Royal or the Queen's Theatre. When I arrived in the following morning, the teacher always said to the class, 'I see the Princess has joined us.' The remark always got a laugh from the class. It was her only joke of the day, so the girls all laughed loudly with what some poet has called 'counterfeited glee'.

I brought Dinah to school and deposited her remains in the harmonium at the back of the class. After a week, she certainly made her presence felt and the stench was dreadful. Several girls complained of feeling sick, so there was a desperate search to find the cause. After a long search, the teacher opened the harmonium and there was Dinah in an advanced sate of decomposition. When Teacher saw Dinah, she screamed, 'Someone get that thing out of here!'

All the girls backed away, so I volunteered and marched out to the bin with Dinah by the tail.

I became Teacher's Pet and she never called me the Princess again.

It's an ill wind . . . .

PADDY POWER

Not Fancied

L ife at the Curragh edge in the early forties was simple. In those days before television or even rural electrification, neighbours and friends dropped in, without invitation, to our home. The caller I disliked most was Abbie — a near neighbour who called daily for her can of milk and all the gossip of the countryside, which she confided to my mother with the loud introduction, 'I have it on good authority that . . .'. The 'that' was usually followed by a low whisper, only meant for my mother's ears and we were left guessing.

It was Abbie who told mother that I had been boxing with Dickie Collins in the Market Square in Kildare before the bus came to carry us home. Both good friends again, Abbie had called on us to 'break' with the aid of her umbrella. Abbie was also the informant when she caught me taking a pull from a Woodbine behind the pier.

Mother maintained that she was a real lady but I'm sure this remark only referred to her gender. She definitely was no oil painting. She was widowed for years and my father, Patsy, claimed that her late husband got the blind pension without further investigation when Abbie answered their door to the knock of the department inspector.

Mick Hanlon was a regular caller on Sunday nights, cycling over from Pollardstown with his carbide lamp on the front and a bulging saddle bag at his rear. He was really mammy's first cousin but was known to everyone as Uncle Mick. He was a bachelor who lived alone and he liked a bit of sweet cake or some of mother's apple tart and a game of 'fifteen' or 'twenty-five'.

Sunday nights had a regular routine. Tea at six was followed by a tidy-up of the kitchen and a look to ensure that the water buckets were full for the morning. A final look around the yard to lock up the hens for the night, and probably a drink for the cow and the pony, left us all set for the family rosary and Joe Linnane's 'Question Time' at quarter past eight. The game of cards for pennies came later.

Uncle Mick usually arrived at eight o'clock. He hung up his coat and hat and placed his lamp on the dresser and Patsy and himself took over the two armchairs at each side of the fire. Only then would Mick tell us to 'go out to see if the cow calved'. This was the signal to examine the saddle bag which was usually full of lovely, sweet apples and a few big cookers for mother to make Mick's favourite apple tart.

However, the programme was ruined one night when the dry battery in the radio conked out. A heat in the oven and a good cleaning of the leads had no effect and silence reigned in Powers' parlour.

We decided to break the monotony by having a competition in the family circle to see who could make the ugliest face and Mick, being the most neutral member, was appointed judge.

Just then Abbie, who had been away all day on a pilgrimage, called for her milk and joined us for her expected chat. All the family imitated monkeys and pulled our jaws and screwed up our eyes to give ourselves as diabolical an appearance as possible and Mick, having given the contest his complete attention, announced the result.

His declaration of 'You win, Abbie' was followed by a great cheer from all the family, but then Abbie protested with great indignation, 'I wasn't playing.'

Patsy, with the tears rolling down his cheeks and failing to disguise the twinkle in his eyes, consoled the reluctant winner with a reward that was surely founded on sad experience of a lifetime in racing: 'Don't worry, Abbie, girl. It's not the first time that a race was won by a non-trier.'

FEARGAL QUINN

One experience I had at the age of five taught me a lot for future life.

I needed an overcoat and my father brought me to a master tailor called Danny McDevitt. He was originally from the Falls Road in Belfast but had now set up business in Dublin.

When I had to go for a fitting, my mother would put me on the No. 7 tram at Temple Hill in Blackrock and I'd ride on that all the way to Nelson's Pillar in O'Connell Street. My father would meet me off the tram and we'd walk to his office nearby in Chapel Lane before going over to the tailor's place.

After the second time we'd done that, my father said to me, 'If I wasn't here to meet you some time, could you find your own way to my office?'

'Of course I could,' I said. 'I'd just walk down Henry Street, take the fourth street on the right and then turn left into Chapel Lane. Sure, I couldn't go wrong!'

The very next time I got off the tram my father wasn't there. I wasn't bothered. Off I headed down Henry Street, counting off the streets. Turn right, turn left — then I got a shock. Chapel Lane wasn't where it should have been!

All my five-year-old's confidence dissolved into tears. But at that very moment, a man from my father's office came up to me and said hello. He took me to the office, and I found that I had counted the streets wrong.

Of course it was all a set-up. My father had sent the man to watch me coming off the tram, and told him not to let me see him unless I got into trouble.

Did he want to boast about his five-year-old who could find his own way around the city? You can be sure he did. But the real reason was that he wanted to instil in his children an ability to have confidence and to stand up for themselves, even at an early age.

I learned from that experience — but I also learned from my father's wisdom in making sure there was a back-up, in case anything went wrong!

NIALL QUINN

I couldn't begin this piece without referring to the VW Beetle. Why? Well, my earliest childhood memories centre around a bright yellow one, registration number 7749 ZH. In fact, I'll go further and build my story around the 'back box' of the said vehicle.

For the uninitiated, this is a reference to the small compartment behind the back seat in all VW Beetles. Normally this is reserved for luggage, pets, hurleys and whatever else one takes on long car journeys. Indeed, this was exactly what our family used the 'back box' for.

Alas, my dear parents also found another use for the 'hallowed ground'. Yep! Every single time we ventured farther than the Naas Road, they dumped me in with at least one cat and trunk-loads of 'Bunty' magazines, destined for two lonely sisters of mine in Presentation boarding school, Ballingarry, Tipperary.

When I say lonely, I must add that it was my mother who complained of their being lonely, not the girls. Thus, every Friday throughout the school calendar, we would load up, head for Lawlor's filling station (this was my first rest), fill the tank and head off for Tipp.

Oh, yes! When someone mentions the Trip to Tipp, it's not rock music or topless backing vocalists that spring to my mind. It's being blamed for the cat's farts and listening to Donncha Ó Dúlaing and his bloody 'Highways and Byeways' for two and a half hours.

'Shut up' or 'Whist' my mother would say. 'He's in Bailieboro today and your cousins might be on!'

Anyway, we wouldn't have gone much past Naas when I'd have fallen into my own little world in the 'back box'.

In recent times, I've often been quizzed on what I feel was my best performance. Well, let me tell you: if Ireland were to win the World Cup and I scored the winning goal, this would just about match the most mundane of games I played in the 'back box'. I played against them all — Christy Ring, Johnny Giles, Brian Mullins, Eddie Keher, Don Givens. They were all either willing team-mates or beaten opposition.

If it was soccer, the game always ended with Billy Bremner pulling me down inside the box and me getting up to score the winner from the penalty spot. In Gaelic, Dublin won every time and I would always compliment big Brian Mullins in mid-field. Hurling nearly always ended up with my supplying the pass for 'Ringy' to score the winning goal for Cork against Kilkenny in Croker! My father had told me that Christy Ring once waved the umpire's green flag himself after scoring a great goal, and this made a big impression on me. To think that I supplied that pass!

I always remember getting as far as Killenaule and realising the convent was a couple of minutes away. I would promptly blow for half-time. I couldn't wait to go back to Dublin. My sisters must have thought I hated them!

It seems funny now, writing about my childhood dreams. Years of adulthood mixed with the realities of professional sport have taken their toll. But every now and then, I manage to get myself 'back' into the 'back box'.

These days, though, there's one big difference — I'd probably listen to Donncha Ó Dúlaing.

CHARLIE REDMOND

Like most people, my childhood years were filled with many happy and varied memories, memories that are now clouded with the passing years. Little was I or my family to know that I would be fortunate enough to play for my beloved county and also lucky enough to play in Croke Park on so many important occasions.

This, however, is in stark contrast to my first appearance there in 1973 for De La Salle, Finglas in the *Cumann na Gael* final. As captain, I was expected to steer our team home to victory. However, as I woke on that morning, I was so sick that I thought I would die. I went downstairs to my mother, who was as excited as anyone on that special day. Her excitement wasn't at the thought of her son playing in the 'Mecca of Gaeldom'. No, it was for the party organised for that evening where she could let her hair down and dance the night away.

As I entered the kitchen on that wet and damp morning, the smell of the 'fry' filled the air. This, however, was sickening to me in my sickly condition.

'What's the matter with you?' she asked.

I explained to her that I hadn't slept at all that night, I had a headache, my stomach was rumbling, my legs were weak, I was suffering from nausea and that I wouldn't be able to play that afternoon. My father was sent for — surely he would know what to do, as fathers were always right, weren't they?

'Haven't got a clue what's wrong with him,' he said. Some father!

'Here, eat your breakfast,' said Mum.

'I'm not hungry.'

And with that I bolted to the loo for the umpteenth time.

'Fetch Mr Campbell. He's a referee. He'll know what to do.'

'Ah,' I thought. 'That's a good move. Another sportsman. He'll definitely know what's wrong with me.'

Referees are never wrong, are they?

'I think he has the flu,' said the man in black.

Not only was he a bad referee, but he'd never make a doctor.

It's now two hours to throw-in, meeting at the school in forty-five minutes. Outside I see other pupils making their way to the school to catch the buses. All of them carrying green flags and sporting hats. My big chance seemingly going away from me. No Croke Park! No leading the team onto the pitch. No coming out of the tunnel. No lap of honour.

I'm still too sick to play. At this stage I'm in bed when one of my sisters enters the room and says very graciously, 'You're only a wimp, afraid to play in Croke Park. You are only suffering from nerves. Ha! Ha!'

It's bad enough to be sick, but having a girl call you a wimp, afraid and nervous — well, I was going to wallop her.

But wait. Our school-master, Mr Ludden, had told us that we'd be nervous, fearful and possibly sick. Now a master, they are always right.

'Drink some hot water,' was what he had told us, 'and that will cure you. This is what the Dublin players take before the matches to overcome their nerves.'

One pint of hot water was duly consumed. A master, no
— a genius, a doctor, a referee, all in one, Mr Ludden.

I have been cured in the nick of time. That famous
antidote, hot water, had sent all the pains and nausea
sprinting from my body. As I grabbed my kit-bag, I ran
towards the school. Here I come, I thought — Croke Park,
leading the team, coming out of the tunnel, lap of honour
— I was going to change the world.

Excitement filled my body and my head was awash with
fanciful thoughts about catching the ball in mid-field,
soloing towards goal, beating player after player and then,
in the final minute, crashing an unstoppable shot to the top
corner of the net for the decisive score. What a day I had in
store.

As I neared the school, I could see the buses and pupils
gathered there. Were they as excited as I was, I wondered.
But as I turned to enter the school gates, I was greeted by
this big sign: GAME OFF.

My world fell apart on the spot. No Croke Park, no
leading the team etc. My mother's world also fell apart
when I told her. However, her disappointment was because
the party was off.

ALBERT REYNOLDS

The Day I Became a Confirmed Teetotaller

I have many fond memories of my childhood days in
Roosky, Co. Roscommon. Warm summer days were
spent swimming in the Shannon with the Hanley
brothers and playing football in the field behind the
house. One particular memory which has remained with me
and which has impacted on my life ever since is the day I'm
going to tell you about.

When I was eight years old, a teacher from Connemara came to say with us for a short while. He didn't arrive empty handed, but brought what one considered the best gift you could receive from the West — a bottle of poitín.

At the time of his arrival, I was competing fiercely in a swimming race down at the Shannon. After the race, I went home bursting to tell my news, that I had won — and of course I was dying with the thirst!

To my disappointment, the house was empty, but sitting on the kitchen table was a great big bottle of water — or so I thought. I knocked it back and suddenly realised that this wasn't regular water.

My mouth was burning.

My stomach was retching.

My head was spinning.

I attempted to get outside for some air but ended up on the floor, having walked into doors, walls and anything else that appeared in front of me.

I lay there until my brother, Jim, found me. He gave me a glass of water to try to revive me, but the only effect this had was that I got drunk again.

When my parents came home and found me, they tried to keep stern faces as they explained what was happening to me. I had heard of the word 'poitín' before, but never really knew what it was. I was certainly experiencing it first-hand now — I was drunk for three days in total.

Maybe all this had a good outcome, because I have never touched a single drop of alcohol since then — until the day of the IRA ceasefire when I was coaxed into having a drop of champagne. To tell you the truth, I'd prefer a cup of tea any day!

RODNEY RICE

odney Rice, aged eight-and-a-half. In a brand new suit. The first ever. Dark green. Still freshly-pressed, sharp creases down the legs of the short trousers. New knee socks too, and brogue shoes. (Well, that's what they called them, though I thought a brogue was a Free State accent.) Little Lord Fauntleroy, according to Aunt Eileen. And, oh so proud.

'Come in and take those good clothes off. We're going up to Kilknock and you'll be out in the fields.'

A sensible woman, my mother.

'No, no, Mammy, I'll be good. I won't get dirty.'

The pride ruled the day; the country cousins should see the finery. A future Louis Copeland customer in the making.

'Well, you'd better be careful.'

Why do mothers always give in?

And off we went to the small village close to Randalstown, Co. Antrim (no metropolis itself) to visit the cousins, once or twice removed.

The city suburbs call on the country. But what a heaven for a child! A white-washed cottage, a turf fire. And outside, a mill ruin, a spring well and a small stream draining into a green-covered flax dam.

Adults have a habit of falling into conversation, of forgetting their duty to hold children to their word.

'Come on, Rodney,' laughed second-cousin-once-removed Hugh. 'Let's play in the field. I have a ball.'

It wasn't the ball that caused the problem. It didn't get time to scuff the brogues. It was the rabbit, disturbed by the human presence. Off it scampered. And us after it. Now we could see it, now we couldn't. And now it appeared across the stream. No problem. There's a plank across the shallow slime. Let's go fast.

Hugh was over. I followed. Was it the still-too-shiny

leather soles, or was it a misplaced foot? Whatever it was, I was face down in the 'sheugh', cold water washing green moss over the new green suit. And the childish tears joined the stream as it fed into the flax dam.

The cousin stood petrified, instinctively knowing there would be an attempt to pass at least a share of the blame. But the music had to be faced.

The shock was fairly evident on the faces of the gathering. But if there was parental anger simmering, it was an early lesson that there's safety in numbers — safety for bold children among a number of adults.

A towel was brought, the turf fire dried the suit, and a 1953-style iron, a red-hot metal block in a metal container, pressed a semblance of respectability into what had been a source of such pride.

But the suit never regained its flair. And a little boy learned that pride does indeed come before a fall.

BARNEY ROCK

One of the many happy memories I have certainly is surrounded by football. It happened on a Christmas morning back in 1967 or 1968. Santa arrived and left, leaving me a Liverpool strip, and my brother Marty a Leeds United strip. So we decided after Mass to try on the outfits and go out in the back garden in the rain and play ball.

But lo and behold, when we went looking for the football, we discovered we had none. So there we were, gear on, and no ball. So I decided to run across the road to a friend's, Billy Conlon's house, to get a loan of his ball, which he gave us.

We had a great game. Liverpool won and we came back like two black men with muck all over us. The mother wasn't too happy, but she knew we enjoyed the presents Santa had left us!

TIM RYAN

Meeting Dan Breen

Donohill in Co. Tipperary, where I was born, is a little-known parish in west Tipperary, close to the Limerick border. It is probably best known as the birthplace of the freedom fighter, Dan Breen, who was born in a small cottage close to my own home.

However, by the time I came on the scene in July 1955, Dan Breen had long left his native parish and was a TD in faraway Leinster House. Due to ill health, he rarely visited his constituency, except at election times. Times are very different now, when a TD risks his or her seat by being absent from base for more than a few days at a time.

So it was from my father and neighbours that I first heard of the exploits of this great warrior, Dan Breen, and his colleagues, notably Sean Treacy, from nearby Sologheadbeg. Like a lot of youngsters growing up in the late fifties and early sixties, one of the first books I ever read was Breen's autobiography, *My Fight for Irish Freedom*. He became my immediate hero.

I was amazed to read of how Breen, Treacy, Sean Hogan and a few others had started the War of Independence on 21 January 1919 at Sologheadbeg stone quarry, just a mile down the road from my home. I was totally familiar with the 'tin house' referred to by Breen in which they had waited for six days for the RIC men to bring the gelignite needed for blasting. The two men were shot dead in circumstances which are still a little unclear, and from that moment on, Breen and the others went on the run, taking shelter first in the Glen of Aherlow.

Later, Breen and Treacy performed even more daring exploits, including the rescue of Sean Hogan, who had been captured by the RIC, from a train at Knocklong station in Co. Limerick. Two more RIC men were killed and both Breen and Treacy were wounded.

Fate finally seemed to have caught up with the rebel pair when they were surrounded in a house in Drumcondra, Dublin, in October 1920. Miraculously, they shot their way out through the British forces, but Breen was wounded yet again.

These exploits were made more real for me by the extra local knowledge of my father and others. While on the run during these troubled times, Breen, Treacy and others used to stay at our house at Grange, Donohill, rather than risk visiting their own homes nearby. As a young boy, my father could remember them arriving in a three-wheel car with a ladder tied to the side for getting past large road craters. He and other young men in the Old IRA kept watch while Breen and Treacy got some badly-needed sleep. I often stared in wonder at the bullet marks on the ceiling in our loft where the RIC had fruitlessly fired, believing the rebels to be hiding inside.

Sean Treacy was shot dead while trying to escape pursuers on Dublin's Talbot Street on 14 October 1920. Breen went on to become a TD, first as a Republican, but later joining Fianna Fáil.

My one and only meeting with Dan Breen was in the mid 1960s at the annual Sean Treacy commemoration in Kilfeacle where he is buried. As an eleven-year-old boy, I was very shy, but proud, when introduced to my hero on an open truck on a cold October Sunday by a neighbour, Josie Ryan, of Grange. Not very diplomatic by nature, Breen muttered a few words, but once he understood who I was, I got special treatment by Breen's standards. I never met Dan Breen again, and he died a few years later in 1969. All I have today are some Christmas cards which he sent to my parents.

Today, as I look down from a somewhat privileged position in the Dáil press gallery, I often wonder what Breen would make of it all. And I wonder, too, what Sean Treacy, a close friend of Michael Collins, would have made of it had he been given a chance.

This year, 1995, is a special one for me. It is the one hundredth anniversary of Sean Treacy's birth and the twenty-sixth anniversary of Dan Breen's death. I hope today's politicians will spare them a moment's thought.

BRUSH SHIELS

Was it all that long ago?

On a place called the Phibsboro Road was an old picture house called the Bohemian (we all called it the Boh), but that was many moons ago. Saturday afternoon, silver sixpence burning a hole in my pocket, I remember my ma's last words to me. She said, 'Hey, Brendan, watch yourself crossing the road at Doyle's Corner. And son, try and be home in time for your tea.'

Those days, Randolph Scott never got shot and Jack Palance dressed all in black. Me and my dad loved Alan Ladd and the young boy who shouted, 'Shane, Shane, Shane, come back!' James Stewart had a Winchester called .73 and John Wayne was in the Alamo, waiting for the cavalry.

Now ma and da, they're both gone.

The Boh is closed, there's no more pictures on. The Phibsboro Road now has traffic jams and the people living there have to keep their doors locked all the time. Sometimes I go over to Phibsboro Park and I look over at where our house once had been and I hear a voice somewhere sayin', 'Hey, Brendan, watch yourself crossing the road at Doyle's Corner. And son, try and be home in time for your tea.'

Those days, Randolph Scott never got shot and Jack Palance dressed all in black and me and my dad loved Alan Ladd and the young boy who shouted, 'Hey, Shane, Shane, Shane, come back!' James Stewart had a Winchester called .73 and John Wayne was in the Alamo, waiting for the cavalry.

Now I play rock and roll, but inside my soul is a cowboy who was always late for his tea.

RAYMOND SMITH

When Little Battleship won the National

My father loved a bet. Never more so than on Grand National day.

This year was different, in the sense that he was not making his own choice from the runners as they were listed in the paper. No. A woman from a neighbouring townland, who had become known for dreaming dreams that in a strange way unravelled events ahead before they ever happened, told how she saw two horses ploughing in a field, one much bigger than the other.

But always the smaller of the two horses was pulling ahead, in front of the other. Down to the end of the field and back. Right to the end of the furrow.

My father studied the field. And decided that the smaller horse had got to be Battleship, who would be ridden by Bruce Hobbs. The bigger horse could only be Royal Danieli. He placed five shillings on 'Battleship', a lot of bread in those days.

Battleship won the National in a field of thirty-six from the 18-to-1 shot Royal Danieli — by a head. At odds of 40-to-1.

My father took us all into Limerick to collect his winnings. I remember his joy as he brought us to the sweet shop and we gorged ourselves on riches we never thought were possible up to then.

We had never heard of champagne corks popping. We didn't care. We were drunk on champagne of a different kind — the champagne of the most glorious, carefree day of our lives when all the world was young and we hadn't a worry in the world.

After that, the Aintree Grand National was always special for me. Could never be otherwise. It represented a world of dreams — but dreams that could be realised.

There are other moments from my childhood that remain indelibly imprinted on my mind — like the night of the great snowfall in Thurles when I went with my father to see the film, Rose Marie, and I thrilled to the singing of Nelson Eddy and Jeanette McDonald. And afterwards, there was a great snow battle in Liberty Square as we were returning home, and my father let me join in.

The freedom of that evening sang in my soul in a strange way that would never die. The blanket of white snow enveloping the broad expanse of the square, under a full moon, spoke of an innocence of a lost era that the children of the present generation can never know.

But I remember Little Battleship most of all, ploughing his own courageous furrow at Aintree, coming home in victory by a head, giving courage to all who are sick and who suffer, and giving me one of the most unforgettable days of my life.

MICHAEL SMURFIT

A Visit to My Father's Factory

I come from a family of eight children and my mind overflows with happy memories of my brothers and sisters. We were very close and the family ties have proven to be consistently strong throughout our grown-up lives. My mother took care of her children in a most outstanding way. It was a full-time job which she performed alone since my father spent little time at home due to the demands of running his own business. We all admired him and appreciated more than anything the moments he devoted to us. I was fascinated by the stories he told, especially those about the paper mill he had built. The factory loomed in my mind like wonderland. I imagined countless workers moving to and fro, fixing machines, lifting heavy equipment. My mental picture stemmed, I expect, from history books about the nineteenth century and the Industrial Revolution. And like many other young boys, when asked about my future career, I answered with remarkable consistency: 'Like my dad, I want to build and run big machines.' And my father used to smile and often add 'I'm afraid you don't know how true your statement is, my son.'

I remember 10 August 1948. It was a nice bright morning, a couple of days after my birthday. My father entered the kitchen where I was eating my breakfast and asked me what I was planning to do that day. I cannot remember what my answer was, but I was clearly puzzled as my father was not one to ask such a question. My father looked at me and smiled, 'You are a big boy now. It is time for you to discover your father's world, which sooner or later will become your own,' and he took me to the mill.

And for the first time I saw the paper machine. It looked enormous and shone brightly. The machine had stopped, as every summer my father changed a few pieces of equipment to upgrade the mill. 'Like a racing car,' he said, 'each season you must be faster or you will never win a single prize. You must fit your engine with the best components.' Tools were clanking around the machinery, the foreman was rushing around frowning. He ran into my father and blurted out that he had a few unexpected problems. One piece had just arrived but its dimensions did not conform to the requirements. As he was talking, obviously distressed by his technical misfortunes, he kept glancing over at me.

He took in my father's comments, but this particular morning, my father was in a very good mood. He introduced me to the foreman, Paddy Tremple, who shook my hand and leaned forward slightly in a very respectful manner. I was told how skilful and competent my father was, and how hard I would have to work if I wanted to take over. I was glowing with pride. My father took me through the mill and introduced me to all the staff. One worker explained to me how they processed the waste fibre into paper. Each time he described equipment, he stressed the fact that my father had chosen and purchased. In my young mind I realised for the first time that this mill had the same father as I did, and ever since, our destinies — that of myself and the mill — have been closely linked.

PAT SPILLANE

My childhood memories are similar to those of any child in rural Ireland growing up during the sixties. Walking to school, little television and longing for the long evenings to arrive so that we could go out and play football in the nearby fields with our neighbours, the O'Sheas and the O'Gradys — tussles of an intensity hardly experienced even in Croke Park. These were full-blooded four-a-side matches, where the physical exchanges in the pursuit of victory often went far beyond the acceptable and defeat left one searching for excuses; going into a sulk and, perhaps, inevitably leading to a campaign of silence where one did not talk to the members of the victorious team for maybe a few days, even if that included a brother or two getting the same treatment as well. I suppose it is from such an environment that champions were made; certainly defeat was not acceptable at any cost.

Maybe we look back at bygone days with rose-tinted glasses and say we will never see the same again. But sadly, rural life as I experienced it during my childhood has changed oh, so dramatically and not, might I add, for the better in many cases. Our little national school where Master Rice and Mrs Rundles looked after us so well is now no longer with us — it is a holiday home for some non-national. Kelly's shop where Geary's penny buns were such a delicacy and Buckley's ice cream are now but pleasant memories.

In once sense, my childhood life was very different from that of most families growing up in rural Ireland. I was brought up in our family public house, living above the bar. There used to the singing and shouting going on underneath my bedroom and I would peer nervously out through the curtain to watch the fighting, which was all too common in those days as neighbours sorted out their disagreements on topics ranging from poaching, cattle, trespassing or rights-of-way. Family outings together were always fairly limited because of the need for Mam or Dad to mind the bar.

Yet one sad memory will always stand out for me. On an October night in 1964, lying in my bed and listening to the commotion and the numerous strange voices in the corridor outside, I was wondering what was going on. I never realised that my father had just died as a result of a massive heart attack, leaving my mother, Maura, to look after four young children, of whom I was the eldest at eight years, and to run the bar single-handedly as well.

My memories of childhood will forever be of the unselfish devotion of my mother as she sacrificed her entire life to the rearing of her children and simultaneously building up the bar business all on her own — never taking a holiday, never leaving the bar for even a single day, ensuring that all the boys got the best education by sending them away to boarding school. (The tears I shed all night in the tower dormitory of St Brendan's College on my first night as a boarder, probably my first night ever away from home, and knowing that the next time I would see Templenoe and the rest of my family would be for a weekend in November.) My mother never had time for television or even entertaining guests.

My childhood memories were, in the main, happy ones, but they will always be dominated by the sacrifices and the hard work my mother did for us. I will be forever grateful.

DAWSON STELFOX

Blackberrying

Picking blackberries is not a necessity any more, but a ritual, the marking of autumn and a reaffirmation of links with the land.

For me, it was an opportunity for adventure, an escape from the regimented streets to the wild tangle of lanes and hedgerows in the foothills of the Mournes. Family and friends; old clothes and wellies; ditches and stone walls; nervous sheep and threatening bullocks . . . the memories blurred now with the passing of time.

September Saturday mornings, up before dawn, breakfast made nauseous by the excitement of anticipation. Packing the peculiar essentials of the art — plastic bags and long, hooked sticks — into the old station wagon with the fold-down rear door that made the perfect picnic table. Friends from down the street crammed into the back, chattering, messin' — squabbling and jostling for position like fledglings in the nest, ready for flight.

Out through early morning mists, suburbia left behind, in the days before the bungalow blitz urbanised the countryside. Clouds dissolved as the sun rose, mountains shimmering in the distance. The thirty miles from Belfast to the Mournes seems as nothing now, but then that journey was an expedition to another world.

For my parents, it was a journey back to the fields and hills of their childhood. For me, it was the start of a journey forward, out into the hills of Ireland and from there to the Alps, the Andes, and eventually the Himalayas and Everest. Although the horizons may have expanded, the excitement, the adventure and the satisfaction of these great mountains have rarely surpassed those early explorations — climbing trees in Belvoir forest, blackberrying around Maghera, Ballyroney and Kilcoo, collecting pine cones with my grandparents in Donard Woods, and later, the first painful but inspiring discoveries of the mountains themselves.

The perfect blackberry — always out of reach. Wild, untamed hedges that had never seen a mechanical cutter. Blackberries the size of plums, full and glistening in the morning dew. The edge of danger, over-balancing into thorny clumps, braving the bullocks, straddling the muddy ditches. Competition too — trying to collect the most, handicapped by greed, the stains of evidence all too obvious on face and clothes.

There is no such thing as the perfect blackberry — the value is in the search. Picking blackberries has evolved from survival to a higher symbolism, of links with the past, our dependence on the natural world and all our subconscious ties, needs and desires.

There is no such thing as the ultimate mountain — the rewards are in the motivation, in the desire, in the quest. Everest, of course, is not just a mountain, but also a symbol.

Success on Everest was less important than the attempt. But of utmost importance is for everyone to have Everests, to have visions, to search. To have your destiny shaped by your own desires, thoughts and actions.

CHARLIE SWAN

I was about six years old when Joe, one of the lads who worked for my father, asked me one afternoon if I wanted to go down to Mrs Casey's shop. Naturally I said yes. We went around the back to one of the stables where a hunter of my dad's was kept. He was called Patrick, a big chestnut horse with a white face and four white socks.

We put the bridle on, then Joe gave me a leg up and jumped up behind me. It took us about ten minutes to get to the shop, as we just walked. When we arrived, Joe got down first. He asked me to jump down and go in for sweets for me and cigarettes for himself.

When I came out, Joe told me to put the sweets on the ground while he gave me a leg back up on Patrick. I had a Brunch ice cream in my mouth. Joe gave me the leg up but when I was up, a dog came sniffing around the sweets on the ground. Joe shouted at the dog to 'shoo, shoo!' but of course he spooked the horse instead.

Patrick took off down the road as fast as he could go. I still had the ice cream in my hand and was trying to pull him up, but it was no good — mind you, I was only six. We were flying up the road, just about to go around a very bad bend, when suddenly, Ken Kavanagh, the local blacksmith, stood in the middle of the road. With his arms wide open, he shouted, 'WHOA! WHOA!' as I clung on for dear life. Luckily, Patrick started to jam on and we eventually came to a stand-still and I jumped off. It took me about five minutes to realise what had happened and I can tell you I was fairly shocked.

The only good thing was that, happily, my ice cream was still in one piece in my hand and Patrick and myself were OK. Joe and I thought it would be best if we kept the whole incident to ourselves, so it was a few years later when we eventually told everyone. They were a bit shocked, but it was too late to be punished.

ALICE TAYLOR

A School Friend

We walked to school
Through the dew drenched fields
Meeting where our paths crossed
At the foot of a grassy hill.
If one ran late, the other
Left a stone message
On the mossy bridge.
He had muddy boots,
A jumper torn by briars
And hair that went its own way.
Trivial details to a mind
That raced amongst the clouds
And followed rabbits down brown burrows.
Gentle hands, twisted by a bad burning,
Reached out towards the birds,
And they perched on his fingers
At ease with one of their own.
Blessed with a mind that ran free
From the frailties of his body
He walked during his quiet life
Close to the gates of heaven.

MAOL MUIRE TYNAN

The Visit

Ella wafted into our lives on a cloud of floral scent and wearing a lemon suit — when they were still called costumes. It was July 1963, four months before her then-untainted champion fell in Dallas.

She was my father's first cousin from Syracuse, Upstate New York, and she gave two weeks' notice of her maiden 'homecoming'. The brevity of her fore-warning typified her unruly, confused system of living but, to look at her, she was the essence of cool order.

After Mass on her first Sunday with us, I asked my mother what a mannequin was and she said a model. That was what a member of the awe-struck congregation had called Ella, our guest and cousin, who, earlier that morning, had dragged from a topsy-turvey suitcase this image of meticulous elegance and sent me under the bed to fetch her nylon stockings.

Her evolution from a state of dishevelled limpness in the morning to exuberant stylishness took approximately twenty minutes. Hypnotised by her ability to produce such a transformation while she hummed and twisted her fair strands into a graceful chignon, I glanced sporadically at the clock and kept an ear for my father's Morris Minor starting up in the yard.

'Do you want some *eau de cologne*, honey?' she would ask, blithely unaware of the exigencies of getting her anywhere on time.

From the moment the telegram heralding her visit arrived, we were caught in a thrilling underflow of excitement in our house. We embarked on a scorched-earth policy, burning what would never be used again, as well as mounds of newspapers, but we kept the 'Better Homes' magazines that Ella used to post to us to indicate to her their value in our eyes.

The burning was followed by washing, then painting and papering. She would sleep in the room we called, for some peculiar reason, the lounge. It looked out on my mother's glorious flower garden with the Devil's Bit mountain beyond.

Her first meal was to be an exercise in Irish culinary classics — ham, of course, brown bread, scones, fruit cake, home-made jam, whipped cream — none of the jolly delicacies that entice children. We need not have worried. Ella brought 'candy'.

My mother and father went to Shannon to collect her from the 6.00 am flight and as she stepped from the car after the drive from the airport, we could hear her bubbling laughter. They were as delighted to be with each other as if they had been together always.

We were scrubbed and plaited and basked in the warmth of her pleasure in seeing us for the first time. She swept us into her fragrant embrace, and we more or less lived there for the next six weeks as we embarked on a rapid bout of day trips to Killarney, Clare, Kilkenny, Dublin — and to 'parties' in the houses of distant cousins in the mountains where she proved her ability as an accomplished *chanteuse* until the early hours.

Ella took endless photographs (we still have them) showing the scrunched-up faces of children adhesed together overlooking Ladies' View.

Her leaving was marked by a period of mourning and depression. Long after she had gone, we still used her vernacular — the sofa became the 'davenport', while nappies were 'diapers'. She used to 'braid' our hair, using 'rubber bands' to secure the plait. When Ella was back in America and the rubber bands were all broken or lost, I went to the shop and asked for rubber 'beans', just as she pronounced it. 'Would jelly babies do?' asked the puzzled shopkeeper.

Twenty years later, I went to see her in Syracuse. She sat on the floor in the basement of her house and fingered through old sepia newspapers of November 1963, as well as the snap-shots taken in Ireland that previous summer — and she cried a river.

MOST REVEREND EAMONN WALSH

Football on the Street

C elbridge, the village of my youth, is a place of many happy memories. While it looked towards Dublin, its outlook was rural, with all the benefits of country life. Football on the street was a favourite pastime in the evenings. The potential for a chase by the gardai and hopefully, a sudden escape, added to the excitement and sharpness of our games and our ability to anticipate danger.

There were few cars or bicycles to contend with, and the convent gate served as ready-made goal posts. On sighting a garda, whoever had the ball ran towards our archway and, with swift precision, threw it over the yard gate. Somehow we realised that footballs, hurleys and sliothars were all safe from confiscation once they were inside the yard. As children we had no idea of what statute granted a safe haven to our treasured sports equipment. We just knew that asylum was down the archway and over the gate.

The escape was not always reached in time, however. I can still vividly see the threadbare tennis ball being confiscated, slowly cut in half by the garda's penknife and returned to me in two gaping halves. In defeat, no words were spoken, no threats made — the two halves said it all. A fair catch was a fair catch.

A few years after I was ordained a bishop, a parcel awaited me when I called to my sister in Celbridge. Inside was a large football and an amusing letter from the same garda, now retired and living happily in my home town. As I read his letter, he said, 'I hope the enclosed football, allowing for inflation, will adequately compensate for your loss forty years ago.'

JOHN WATERS

The Tunnel of Trees

There's more to memories than meets the memory. There are things you remember, and things you remember. That is to say, there are different levels of remembering. Beyond the level of conscious recall there are things which lodge within you, body, mind and soul, in a special way, and for a special purpose and reason. These memories are especially strange because they have absolutely no resonance at the conscious level. There is no 'point' to them, no punch line, no joke, not event a decent anecdote. They are more like tastes or smells which almost do not exist, but which burn inside of you as though seeking to repeat themselves just one more time.

I think this is what memory is, a set of early visions which, by their mystery and magic, drive you ever onwards in a quest to re-experience them. You never do, of course, but that's all right. The point is in the hunger these moments leave behind, a glimpse of heaven or hell, or both, which gives meaning and purpose to all future journeys. Through your life, they act as unconscious guides, drawing you to certain things, places and people, and away from others. They help you to seek out a home, in the broader sense of a place in the world, in nature and the human community. Behind all such searching are the colour, taste, texture and sounds of moments of magic or happiness which go beyond the material.

One such moment from my childhood concerns one of the annual summer holidays I spent with my sister Marian in my Aunt Teresa's house in Cloonyquin, just a couple of hundred yards from where Percy French was born. From all such summers, only stray moments survive, and these often for no discernible reason. And yet, from time to time, I see traces of them in places I have chosen to live, and in things which give me a kind of pleasure which is disconnected from any material or even conventionally emotional source.

This special moment is associated with the evening we arrived in Cloonyquin, and with the stretch of road which went past the house towards the avenue of what used to be French's, away from the crossroads a mile on the other side. This stretch of road was shrouded in trees, and there is something about that tunnel of trees which lives with me yet and seems to mean something more than I have been able to perceive. The trees are still there, but even if they weren't, they would survive in my head. There is a vaguely similar stretch of road close to where I now live, and I go there whenever I need to feel a particular kind of strangeness.

I remember us walking through the tunnel in the dusk in search of our Uncle Jimmy, the trees on either side of the road alive with the racket of the recent rain. This moment is frozen forever in my consciousness, in a manner beyond conventional recall or word or image. Droplets tripping from the towering treetops that met overhead in the centre of the road's air-space, buffeted from leaf to twig to branch as they tumbled downwards, oblivious of the consequences of their impending contact with the ground, slapping and tutting and sighing and moaning as they spat down from their temporary halting places. The sound of drops could be heard both separately and in unison with the others — on the one hand a plop, a plip, a determined round splat; on the other a hissing, streaming, torrent of sound, like a living device for distilling and delaying the sensation of falling rain. All around were sudden cracks and sighs, as if the world might soon awake from a deep sleep. Away in the depths of the trees were the shapes and shadows of plants I knew but could not name. One like a strange crouching bird that seemed to be alive, another with a sharply featured triangular-shaped leaf as green as a front door. In the pockets of light beneath where the tunnel's roof remained open to the sky, small clouds of midges had gathered to gossip silently before darkness fell, like pockets of displaced cloud looking for the exit to go home.

Straight ahead on the far side, as the road curved into the climb towards the hayfields and the sun, was the hungry gate of an old tumble-down house where two elderly sisters lived. The little house stood in its fairy-tale grandeur silhouetted against the western sky, now clearing momentarily before capitulating to the darkness, the sun making a stain of redness that seemed to seep through the house like a hand through a light bulb.

One of the sisters stood at the gate, staring deep into the tunnel as though she and she alone were responsible for the hubble-bubble of the weeping trees. As we emerged into what was left of the light, we caught sight of her together. She stood immobile in the gateway, watching us as if we were animals come out to forage for food in the aftermath of the downpour. She made no move either to retreat or acknowledge our presence. Nothing would convince us that she was not a witch.

Get on your marks. Get set. Go. We ran like the wind out of the dark tunnel, past the placid gaze of the witch at the gate who watched with the detachment of a statue, her head only swivelling remotely to follow our progress round the curve of the road. As we slowed with the resistance of the hill, I cautiously glanced backwards to make sure she had remained standing inside the gate. I caught the witch's eye and she raised her hand in a sweeping motion, as though to summon up the forces of darkness in our wake.

In her fingers she held a lighted cigarette, a wand of white and fire.

At once we heard a gathering sound like a cloud of locusts, but really just the whirring of an approaching bicycle, tearing with the gradient of the hill. Our Uncle Jimmy, dressed in clothes as dark as the heart of the tunnel of trees, astride the black bike, came out of the by-now vague space between the ditches with the certainty of belonging. The humming of the bicycle mingled with the discourse of the tumbling droplets in the tree-tunnel's million leaves, like a stream of running water or something live that couldn't settle, as though the bicycle were as part of this as anything, as though it had learned the language of this place and belonged here even more than the prodigal rain. He lifted me onto the bar of the black bike and helped Marian to get astride the carrier. As though our weights made no difference, he pushed the bike forward and began walking it back towards the house. As we drew level again with the gate of the house where the witch stood watching, he let go of the right-hand handlebar and lifted his cap to the witch at her gate, the cigarette clasped tightly in her lips, her eyes all but closed against the smoke.

'Well, Mary Kate,' he said.

'Hello,' said the witch.

She spoke without taking the cigarette from her mouth. She seemed not to know it was there at all, never mind think to shake the ash off it. I watched it waggle slightly, a clue to the source of the hoarse hello, and waited forever for the moment when the ash would fall off. It grew and grew until there was more ash than cigarette, then hardly anything but ash at all, like a thin tongue.

Jimmy and the witch talked for maybe five minutes, short bursts of fire across the gate, about the rain and the damage it was doing, about how the hay would be lost and the turf not found, about how even the flowers in the witch's garden were scalded with water. We listened silently. Then he kicked a pebble from under the wheel of the bicycle and said good-night to the witch and we went home, leaving her standing at the gate, lighting our way to the end of the tunnel of trees with the dying glimmer of her cigarette.

HARRY WHELEHAN

Tootin, the Loving Gosling

One of the luckiest days of my life was the day Molly came to look after me. While I was then too young to know what was happening, being only a few weeks old, I have come to know and love Molly all through the fifty-one years of my life. She came to help my mother to mind me when I was born, as my mother already had three other children.

As Molly cared for me and looked after all my needs, I loved her gentleness and her kindness. She came to know all my likes and dislikes and devoted herself to making me happy in every possible way. Of course my mother and father and brothers and sisters also loved me, and I loved them, but in a most special way, Molly and I belonged to each other and, indeed, we still do.

When I started school at the age of four, Molly was no longer needed to look after me and she returned to her home, deep in a remote part of the countryside where her mother and Paddy, her old uncle, lived on a small but beautiful farm. The day Molly left us to return home, my father brought me with him for the drive in the car. I had not been to Molly's home before, nor had I met her mother or Paddy until that day.

Never before had I been so deep in the countryside, way in off the road. We finally came to Molly's home which was situated in the middle of the farm. The house was beautiful in its simplicity and in its setting. We approached in the car across a huge field which led to the front yard. There we met Bran the sheepdog, the white gander, the grey goose Muss, the tabby cat Dolly, the pet cow, and about fifteen red hens and a large red cock.

When Molly got out of the car, all of the animals were clearly delighted and happy to see her back home again. Paddy was at the door and gave us a great welcome. Molly's mother was in bed. I did not know until then that she was too old and too ill ever to leave her bed. We went in to meet her. She was lovely, and it was great to see how happy it made her to have Molly back home. She slipped a threepenny piece into my hand when she shook hands with me — I had never before been given a present of money. She told us how delighted she was to have Molly back to mind her and turning to me, she said that she hoped that I would not miss Molly. As soon as she said this, I burst into tears, because only then did I realise that I might never, ever see Molly again in my whole life. It was at that moment that I realised just how strongly attached to Molly I had become.

All the way back to Mullingar I was in tears, and for days and weeks, I could not be consoled. Finally, my parents said that they would see if Molly would allow me to visit her occasionally.

Molly was thrilled with this idea. As a result, I used to spend my school holidays at that lovely farm with this special family and all their lovely animals.

The memories I have of these times are the most precious of my whole childhood. The fields, the meadows, the hay-making, cutting the turf in the bog, collecting eggs, collecting mushrooms, the country smells outside and the smell of home-baking, country butter and cooking on the open fire inside the house. The smell of the oil lamp at night as we sat by the open turf fire and talked of today and tomorrow and of people and of times past. In all of these great holidays, I had only one episode of deep unhappiness by which I was devastated and seriously upset and frightened.

One spring, the goose laid an egg, just one egg. And for some reason, neither she nor the gander would sit on it or try to hatch it out. Seeing this, Molly took the large goose egg and put it under a hen which was hatching some eggs of her own. The hen took the egg into her nest and treated it with the same care as all of the others she was hatching.

The chicks and gosling were duly hatched and the hen, who was very astonished to find a gosling among her chicks, refused to look after the little gosling. She continually pushed it out from among her chicks and into the cold. Molly took the poor little rejected gosling and gave me the responsibility of minding it — she showed me how to feed it with milk and oatmeal and how to keep it warm. I could not believe how quickly it grew and how soon it was able to walk. I called it Tootin, and to my amazement, it began to answer to its name and to follow me around the house. If I was going outside the house, I would wrap it in a woolly jumper and carry it under my arm. At night, I would put it in a box near the fire with a hot water jar wrapped in a towel for it to snuggle up to. It was a very curious affair, but we became totally attached to each other.

By the time my holidays ended, Tootin was able to follow me around outside the house and even down to the pond where he was just about able to swim and duck his head under the water. I really loved this little yellow, fluffy friend who showed me as much affection as I showed to him.

As the holidays ended, I dreaded having to leave him to go back to school, knowing that I would not see him for three months until I came back to Molly's during the Christmas holidays. I picked him up and gave him a big kiss. When I put him down, he bowed his neck up and down six or seven times, shook his head and wagged his tail as if to say, 'See you soon, my friend.' He was still all yellow and fluffy because his feathers had not yet begun to grow. He was, however, becoming less dependent on me and so I knew that he would survive until I came back to Molly's during my next holiday.

When I returned to Mullingar and to school, each day I thought not just of Molly, but of my dear friend, Tootin. I was so proud of how I had become his friend and how he had become mine.

When the next school break came, I could not wait to go back to Molly's, not just to meet everybody, the animals and the neighbours, but especially to continue my great friendship with Tootin.

When we arrived at Molly's, my father let me out of the car. I first went running round the yard and then down to the pond to find my friend. To my astonishment, there he was, fully fledged in white feathers and with a red beak, grazing away with the goose and gander beside the pond. He was fully grown and almost the size of his father. As I rushed forward, calling his name and reaching out towards him to scoop him into my arms, he faced me, stretched out his neck towards me and began to hiss viciously and flap his wings in a threatening way as he rushed towards me in a most aggressive way. I was stunned and alarmed and immediately turned tail and ran like mad back towards the house and car, with Tootin in hot and close pursuit.

Molly, Paddy and my father came rushing to my rescue and managed to repel the attack with difficulty. I was in bits, frightened and completely disillusioned by this experience. I was so sad, and I began to distrust all of the animals with whom I had always been so friendly. My confidence in myself and in the animal world was shattered. I felt I had lost all of my friends and I became very fed up with life. Being in Molly's family lost a lot of its purpose and pleasure for me, something which I thought could never happen.

However, Molly quickly came to the rescue and, slowly and painstakingly, day by day, she explained to me how each of us as persons, and each creature and animal by reason of its own special nature, can only have a certain amount of 'nature' in common — we each need our own space and our own freedom to develop and function in accordance with

God's plan. We must respect that domestic animals and, indeed, wild animals, are intended to be as they were created and they cannot become human. Some of them might have a special insight or a relationship with a human or an animal from a different species, but eventually, all creatures, including us humans, must maintain the characteristics of our own breed in order for the world to continue to be such an interesting place, evolving as nature intended.

This theme of Molly's continued throughout the holidays as each day she took an example from the animals around the farm, her old pet cow, Dolly, the calves, the chickens, the lambs, the kid goat and even tadpoles and butterflies that she had had the pleasure and experience to love and befriend while they were young and dependent on her, and before they were able to stand on their own feet among their own species.

This is how I came to realise that animals and all creatures must be reared to achieve a level of independence, in the same way as human children eventually grow up and leave the nest.

By the time my holiday was over, I had come to look, not with fear, not with sadness nor with resentment, on Tootin, but I regarded him with the greatest of pride and with great pleasure because my helpless, orphaned little gosling had grown up to the point where he stood proudly beside his mother and father in their own special world. To look at him strut around the yard, he was as fine a gander as was ever reared by man or goose.

Thanks to Molly, I had the experience of three great and powerful emotions during that six-month period — love, fear and pride, not to mention acceptance, rejection and reconciliation!

GORDON WILSON

The Inspector

Icould bring you to the very floor-board in the schoolroom where this incident happened. I was ten years old at the time, in my last year at Manorhamilton primary school.

Our teacher, Mrs Boyd, lived in terror of the inspector from the Department of Education. He was a big-shot, descending on us every year from Dublin. His brief was not only to see were the young scholars making the grade but did the teacher cut the mustard too. Mrs Boyd's greatest fear was that her pupils would make a fool of her in front of this important visitor. As there were only thirty of us in the entire school, we would all come under close scrutiny. So, of course, Mrs Boyd had us shaking in our shoes with fear of her and of the inspector.

On that day in 1938 when the inspector visited our little class of five, he chose geography as the subject with which to torment us.

'In what towns in Ireland are boots and shoes made?' he asked.

'Dundalk,' answered the first lad.

Mrs Boyd smiled.

'Carlow,' said the second.

Mrs Boyd glowed.

'Killarney,' said I.

'Oh, no,' the inspector shook his head sadly.

Mrs Boyd's smile withered. She looked at me as much as to say, 'Stupid boy, who ever heard of shoes made in Killarney?' I was in for a slating when the inspector left.

Now, my father sold boots and shoes in his drapery shop, as Mrs Boyd well knew. And of course, the inspector did not. When I went home for lunch that day, I told my father the story of the inspector's visit.

'Wait a minute,' my father said. Rising from the table, he went downstairs to the shop and returned carrying an invoice. 'R. Hilliard & Co., Boot & Shoe Manufacturers, Killarney' was written across the top of the page.

'Bring that back to school and show it to the inspector,' he said.

With great temerity I approached Mrs Boyd that afternoon and offered her my piece of paper.

'Well,' she beamed, quickly spotting an opportunity to take the credit herself. 'Wait till I show this to the inspector.'

The inspector looked at the invoice, then at me, and said, 'This is the first time in forty years of inspecting schools that I've been put right by a pupil.'

And I was in Mrs Boyd's good books for a day or two after that!